SKY IS THE LIMIT

SKY IS THE LIMIT

Skyrocket Your Sales & Set Yourself Apart from the
COMPETITION *with the Influence of God's* **CREATIVE** *Power.*

TERESA TAYLOR

iUniverse, Inc.
Bloomington

Sky is the Limit
Skyrocket Your Sales & Set Yourself Apart from the
Competition with the Influence of God's Creative Power.

iUniverse books may be ordered through booksellers or by contacting:

iUniverse
1663 Liberty Drive
Bloomington, IN 47403
www.iuniverse.com
1-800-Authors (1-800-288-4677)

Because of the dynamic nature of the Internet, any web addresses or links contained in this book may have changed since publication and may no longer be valid. The views expressed in this work are solely those of the author and do not necessarily reflect the views of the publisher, and the publisher hereby disclaims any responsibility for them.

Any people depicted in stock imagery provided by Thinkstock are models, and such images are being used for illustrative purposes only.

Certain stock imagery © Thinkstock.

ISBN: 978-1-4502-8886-6 (sc)
ISBN: 978-1-4502-8887-3 (ebk)

Printed in the United States of America

iUniverse rev. date: 02/23/2011

In memory of the two fathers in my life.

Guillermo and Alfredo.

Thank you for your love and encouragement.

You will never be forgotten.

TABLE OF CONTENTS

CHAPTER TWELVE

CHAPTER THIRTEEN

FOREWORD

Everybody is *in* sales. We all find ourselves selling our ideas, persuading others on our initiatives, and having to convince people of our skills and abilities. Whether it is a job interview or while meeting that special person, we have to somehow 'pitch' ourselves to others; so I didn't have to *work* in sales to find this book inspiring, and timely.

I have been a friend of Jon and Teresa Taylor for over twelve years, so I can talk about the circumstances they both faced from the early stages of Teresa's arrival to the United States from her hometown in Colombia. It was interesting to see that she did not shrink from the barriers of limited experience, and the challenges of handling a second language, while stepping off in a new environment. She started a new career as if it were meant to be. It was inspiring to observe how she took her new professional sales job seriously from the beginning, and has made the most of it over the past ten years.

I am now witnessing a new stepping-stone in her life. Millions of individuals have been heard to say, *"I should write a book!"* And millions do...even when at times, it is not exactly those who only dream and talk about it. Hard-working creative people make it happen.

In this welcome volume, Sky is the Limit, Teresa, a brave friend, writes about a field of endeavor that is flooded with solid How-To books, including e-books, pamphlets, and training courses filled with hype and hope. It was her audacity, bravery, and commitment that compelled me to offer to work with her to transform the original text without making it my own. Words and phrases can be exceedingly precious to a writer, and writing in a language other than one's mother tongue can present some daunting challenges. Allowing for 'precious' language was the hardest work for me, but I reminded myself that it is <u>her</u> message; and it seemed important to at times remind her that she had already completed the book; and that we were simply making adjustments, so the project would be easier for her readers to take in and use.

If I should say there were no moments of struggle, I'd be telling you a lie! But the strength, charm, and confidence that Teresa brought to the process made it a labor of light.

The husband of whom she proudly writes worked in one of my companies for many years, and that effortlessness she admires was welcome in his performance then. He is an outstanding award-winning sales manager. We remain friends to this day.

Her representation of the Competitive and the Creative as poles and as processes, appealed to me, as did her desire to weave in the threads of Scripture to tie the entire project together. Having worked in the creative mode from my childhood, and having developed a strong respect for Scripture, and the timeless principles contained therein, it was easy to understand why she so wants to get her message out to people, including salespeople, around the world. It can change lives. After you have read this creation, and tried some of her recommendations, let her know how they have affected your personal and professional experience.

I am honored to have played a small role in this project, and I feel confident that we accomplished our original objective, and hopefully much more.

Dr. Cedric E. Davis
Editor

"Odd how the creative power at once brings the whole universe to order."

Virginia Woolf

INTRODUCTION

My Breakdown

You should know that this book is a case. It is the case for the influence of God's Creative power in life—but most of all it is the description of how such influence has exponentially increased my sales production. An influence that has allowed me to leave feelings of stress and struggle behind, while helping me reach a more balanced state of mind; one in which I am happier and able to succeed in a more relaxed way.

I stumbled upon a variety of opinions and reactions during early efforts to relate my personal experience using the Creative process to others. While some of the feedback was very positive, especially from those ready for a change, I did also meet an expected level of skepticism. My all-time favorite remark so far is, *"Sales and...relax!? Well, I don't think so! Those two words do not go together."*

My response, however, has always been the same. *Yes, it is possible!* Joy, flow and success, are only part of the results obtained by working within the proper course of action. That is precisely what *Sky is the*

1

Limit is all about—It is the expose of the two main processes that each one of us inevitably experience ….and until today, it was all happening without much knowledge, or with minimal awareness…but that is all about to change!

I have worked in sales as a Cruise Consultant , for over ten years; and if you are like me, I am sure that at the end of any given day you have at least once marveled at how awesome that day was, and still wondered why yesterday was such a disaster. What did you do today, that was different from yesterday? Better yet, why is it that everyday cannot be like your best day? It all feels like Russian roulette. We can't help but feel 'lucky' when the day brings the desired number of sales, or at least the right kind of customers, but since it doesn't work out that way all the time, it is always much easier to blame it on traffic, the economy, your spouse, and why not?...even on the moon.

The reality is that majority of times we are searching in all the wrong places. We tend to blame it all on the externals, when the truth is that everything that is needed for success is within us.

So, why is it a case? Well, have you ever seen lawyers build one? They first must know the law that applies to the specific situation. Second, before they even pick the case, they must get the information about the issue at hand. At some point, an evaluation is needed to determine the mental state of the defendant or the victim. Though some of them start their defense with little or no evidence, it is safe to say that, the more they dig, the more they find. This book is about letting you know what I found.

The laws…are laid out in the Bible (See Appendix A). The crime is described as heightened levels of stress. The culprit: Following the wrong process. The victim: Me. And the mental condition, you may ask… Well, I was pleading insanity. An even more painful reality is that I am not alone. Millions of other professionals in the world do fall victim to the same circumstances; especially, in sales, where the widespread conception from the employee's point of view is that it could be an 'uphill battle;' while the point of view from the client's prospective, does not always place us in the best light.

But allow me to first tell you about me and about the circumstances that got me here. Allow me to tell you about the two specific processes that have undoubtedly changed my perspective. Better yet, let me tell you how I came about finding the solutions and answers that can potentially change the way you view sales.

Well, for starters, I am from Colombia. A country famous for its coffee…and yet, I have to confess, I cannot stand it! But why is it that after working in sales for just a few years it had become my lifeline?

People around me in the office drank it in the Big Gulp cups from 7-Eleven; so I guess I decided to get into the trend and give it an honest try. I soon started to notice how the java jolt made me feel energetic, and in some curious way, it prepared me to face the day. Despite my resistance to making it a morning routine, it was actually starting to become harder and harder to get through the day without it.

Maybe, if I had drunk my usual cup of Joe on the morning of June 14, 2007, I could have avoided what became a memorable day, and not for good reasons.

The day started out like any other. As usual, I got up on the right side of the bed. I picked what to wear in the last minute, and remember leaving out the door in a rush. I know for a fact that I wasn't thinking about much of anything while on my way to work, other than how Republicans and Democrats really needed to get their act together, and put the economy back in place; based on the back and forth discussion on the radio talk show I still tune in to every morning. I'd say it was the same routine for the past few years…so I can't truly say I saw it coming. I guess I was ok with denial. In the end, the reality is that pressure built up took control, and before that day was over, I looked back and found myself without a job.

The atmosphere at work, on the sales floor was great and even fun at times. We all looked forward to the next contest. It was exciting to compete against each other for rewards, incentives, and off course, bragging rights to the highest sales transactions. In addition, we were divided into teams, and we were encouraged to prove which team was best. The company displayed each employee's profit and every team's achievement in an effort to exhibit the top producers. I personally thought it was convenient. At least I knew whom I was up against.

I could always appreciate efforts to push us to be better, produce more, and become the best for the sake of higher profitability. It could only help us. I personally wanted a bigger paycheck every month. At least that was my thinking, and a very rational one by many standards, but something was about to make that day different. I was about to realize that what I was consciously processing as fun and challenging was actually having the opposite effect within. Too bad, it became clear only after it hit a breaking point. By then, it was already too late.

I felt exhausted. It was as if I had burnt out, and there was no fuel left in me. All kinds of thoughts were running through my mind; some saying, selling wasn't for me anymore, and others that found my commission profits, and paycheck no longer acceptable. Having to produce more to reach my personal goals was becoming strenuous, but having to do so, while I did not have the energy, was definitely starting to take a toll on me.

So by noon, I was already thinking it would be a great idea to quit. I have to admit, I have had brighter ideas in the past, but suddenly, I was willing to leave behind seven years worth of seniority, benefits, accomplishments, and experience for something else.

I had no backup plan, but at that time, just having freedom sounded like one. I was determined to go in a search for 'greener pastures,' maybe even start my own business. Get my control back! I was determined to live a life with no added pressure from the sales world. That was it! I was not going to take it one more minute!

Without further thought, and in a flash, I got up from my desk and went to my boss' office. I told him I was leaving, and that I was there just to say good-bye. No letter of resignation, and forget about the standard six weeks' notice... It was time for me to leave.

I could see the shock in my boss' face, and with reason. I wasn't a bad employee, and at that moment, it was obviously not his intention to let me go; so he did try to reassure I did not have to. But I wasn't about to hear anything! I had made up my mind. I was leaving, and there was no turning back, not even to pick up a thing. There was certainly not going to be a cardboard box with a teddy bear on one side, and a plant on the other. It was just me out of the door. I felt brave enough to face any consequences, and all I wanted then was to get as far away from sales... and as fast as possible.

Well, that day was finally over...but the aftermath was far from it. I soon realized that I was only "brave" for those frantic twenty minutes that it took to fire myself. Fast-forwarding twenty-four hours, I was fully back to my senses, and it all felt like a hangover. What did I just do!?

Suddenly, it was all coming back to me... Despite my recent thoughts, I had been profitable and somewhat successful; so what went wrong? At that moment, only one thing was for sure... I had all the freedom I wanted – yep!

It was time to face the music. I had to tell my husband, and even my closest friend about the unexpected turn of events, and about my new job status. In all sincerity, I thought I was about to hear a handful, but surprisingly that wasn't the case. What my best friend said meant a lot to me then (…and even more now, as I'm writing this book). In his own words, *"Everything happens for a reason."* Nonetheless, it was my husband's seemingly simple advice that made a world of difference.

While I was commenting on how worried I was that I had left my job without much planning to start a new one, he simply added, *"Don't worry! God blesses faith, not fear."* His response resonated with me, but I had to wonder for a moment what God had to do with my impulses and career decisions. After all, I did fail to think of Him enough to include Him while I had a job. How dare I look for Him now, only because I don't!? But that question did manage to linger long enough in my mind to inspire me to seek out answers… and it is precisely what I found out what I humbly present to you within the pages of this book.

My Breakthrough

My husband also worked in sales; and though I have always recognized his positive qualities, I have to admit that his sales approach, was definitely not one of the aspects on the list. I love how much we both enjoy going to the movies… a lot, which is no shorter than our own version of a compulsive disorder. And I love his efforts to surprise me with the occasional surprise trip or special dinner reservations. But it was while he wasn't even trying, that he became a true inspiration and the motivation for this book.

Some of our friends say we are made for each other, and I do believe our personal lives seem to be somewhat in-sync; but it wasn't until I had the time to pause and reflect that I was able to recognize that professionally, we were miles apart from each other. That was my personal observation after evaluating the disparity between the results we both attained at work, as well as our level of effort. For starters, I was spending hours devouring books in a quest to find the perfect sales process that could help me improve my sales skills and results. It was a non-stop search, since I never really knew what I was looking for; so, while my husband was easily achieving all his monthly goals without much apparent effort, I, was becoming more robotic each day and undoubtedly more stressed.

That surprising advice he gave me right after I quit my sales job would seem rather simple and generic, but it was actually a sneak peak peek into his mentality. The reality was that each book I read, one after the other, was becoming more technical and barely motivational; and at some point, they all felt more like a diversion. I soon realized that all I had to do was pause, and notice. The best answer was already living in my house.

One of those nights while I was at home (needless to say, jobless)… Jon, my husband, arrived from work with all kinds of business cards, and a huge grin on his face. I was afraid to ask, but of course, I had nothing else to do.

He started telling me what an exciting day he had at work. I was sitting (…I did say jobless, right?) in front of him, hearing him talk about all the people he had met at work that day. He kept going on about how he had met a jazz musician, a sports coach, and a bank manager; while without missing a beat, commenting on how much I would have enjoyed meeting the coach's wife, because she was Puerto Rican, and he thought the two of us would get along great.

At some point in his monologue, I felt the urge to get up and leave… I thought he was being insensitive on purpose; but moments later, I was very glad I didn't. I was able to overcome my personal feelings to notice something much greater. Pettiness aside, I was starting to realize there was somehow much more to it.

Then it happened! Something hit me like a ton of bricks. I had seen the business cards all around the house, and at that point, I couldn't help but wonder how I failed to notice similar clues before. For example, he always looked relaxed and upbeat, while I became more frustrated each day, and the majority of times I found myself returning from work exhausted and drained, while he would come back from work more energized than when he left.

I planned right there and then to give my husband more attention. I was starting to wonder if he was really coming back from work. I really do trust him, but the way he was acting didn't make much sense. If he was in sales, just as I was, he wasn't supposed to be all that excited… all the time… was he? I felt I was facing a constant struggle. One that involved lowering prices to remain *competitive* and conversations that never went past the typical ex-wives topic, and the local weather. What was he doing right, that I wasn't?

Very discretely, I started to stop by the store to see him while he was at work. I was hoping to witness firsthand his interaction with customers and peers alike. On several occasions, I saw people coming into the store asking for him by name. He always kept a sincere smile on his face; he exuded a certain confidence in his ability to show the product. He showed his customers that he cared, by always doing his best to help; and just as if he was born with 'it,' on an overwhelming number of occasions, he closed the deal right on the spot.

Customers responded very positively to his demeanor, and to the different qualities and traits, he displayed. Their conversation flowed in a very relaxed manner, so the result was a very effective encounter. That is how he got customers comfortable enough to give him not only information about their professions, hobbies, and even their spouses' names and nationalities, but their credit card numbers as well.

I was eager to learn more about his approach, so I decided to get more answers directly from him… all without him knowing, of course. If he ever so slightly got any indication that I was trying to learn anything from him, I would have never heard the end of it. Knowing the way he is, he would have become very practical, while making every effort to over-explain it. I sure did not want to deal with his ego.

So after I snatched him from work with the excuse of a lunch break, and after ten minutes of random chitchat, trying to mask my real interest for specific information…I decided to finally get to business and jump to the first question that came to mind. I asked him if after much effort there was ever a worry of losing business to co-workers or competitors. Barely turning away from his spinach chicken salad, and while shrugging his shoulder as if I had just asked him a rhetorical question, he simply responded: ***"Why would they need to go anywhere else?"***

"What? Why would they need to go anywhere else? Now you are just trying to be cocky, right? Are you kidding me? Who told you to be that confident, especially in these times? And why are you asking me, darling? Don't you think I can be confident in my abilities too? I, too, am good at what I do, you know?" Well, I did not say any of that…but I was sure thinking it.

One thing was certain: His response didn't lower my desire to learn more about his approach, or to ask fewer questions, for that matter. My curiosity continued as strong as ever. Confidence, flow, high results, good communication, repeat business, relationships built in the process, and doing it all with such a good attitude…?!

Coffee had become my energy source, but I was curious to know, what his was. Whatever the answer, I was convinced it was worth the search… but where do I start? So far, the best I could do was to theorize. I obviously didn't have any information other than my observations to rely on, and so I wondered.

I came up with my first hypothesis. I called it, the *Polarity Theory*. Based on discrepancies between his results and mine, and after comparing his amazing flow in the process with my… failed job status, I was starting to grasp the idea that there were possibly *two different sides* when it comes to sales… and suddenly, I was getting the eerie feeling that I was on the 'wrong' one.

It was only a theory, but looking at the world around us, it somehow made sense. Regardless of what we do or feel, there has always been a co-relation between two opposite poles or tendencies. One represents what we may categorize as positive while the opposite stands on the negative.

You see, since we were kids, our parents always tried to teach us *right* from *wrong*. We grew up watching movies that emphasized the fight between *good* and *evil*. *Love* and *hate* are choices we face every day, and choices that can potentially make the difference between *peace* and *war*. There are countless examples of opposites—*Night* and *day*; *happiness* and *sadness*; *black* and *white*; *up* and *down*; *pros* and *cons*…and off course my favorite, sweet and sour.

The theory would somehow help explain the results accomplished within each approach. It would become obvious that the wealthy and content salesperson is not standing at the same end of the spectrum as the one who lacks and struggles. Now, if I could only figure out the way each individual arrives at that particular position…

For a moment, I felt as if I was getting somewhere, but that theory didn't provide any answers for the so-called *energy source?* If I truly wanted to venture into polarity in order to find explanation for some of my queries, how would I explain the importance of the active presence of both positive and negative in some of the most common (artificial) energy sources we depend on daily?

Whether it is the kind of battery that gets the car running, or the kind that gets that famous bunny in the commercials going, they both rely on what is called electrical polarity. For a battery to generate the energy, both negative and positive must be present. Electrons flow from the negative pole to the positive pole. We get a glimpse of that fact when we see the plus and minus signs on each battery, and good luck trying to flip channels with your remote control if the battery is not placed in its proper alignment.

Was my theory crumbling? And if that was the case, what could put it back together?

In the meantime, other ideas and theories can pop into anybody's mind on a day-to-day basis; like the one that makes it easier to assume that employees, who remain at the top of the charts, are somehow related to the top executives of the company, and because of that, leads are constantly sent their way. While that theory will never be fully discarded, I think it is time we find the actual reason why in many cases certain sales professionals can be more successful than others.

Is it really, because they happen to know the right people? Did they happen to read a better book? Or should we give in to the popular belief that some are born with 'it,' while it is just tough luck for the rest of us?

In the following pages, you will be reminded that there is certainly more to it than meets the eye; and becoming more aware of which process we choose to follow could make a powerful difference between *success* and *failure*, or *flow* and *struggle*. What follows, could be the theory that puts it all together.

"The creative process is not controlled by a switch you can simply turn on or off; it's with you all the time" (Alvin Ailey 1931-1989)

This is a modest book. Nowhere has it promised to make you a 'super-selling machine.' One of its purposes is to simply identify and unleash not only the potential that already lies within you, but also the creative abilities given to each one of us. Abilities that can be often overlooked due to our own conscious or unconscious decisions to react to external factors, while ignoring the internal.

A house is not built from the roof down and the foundation of a tree is not its flowers. It is what we cannot see or what lies beneath the surface, that ultimately determines if a structure is built to withstand the test of time…or not. It is by the same concept that I remind you that either created by God or man, it all begins from its foundation; it all starts from the inside.

Awareness is the key to mastering the potential that lies within us; but how can we truly master it, if we are not reminded of its power?

Great sales books in the market may provide you with more technical, but still effective selling techniques; books written by authorities in the profession, and filled with expert selling advice that I do recommend you apply when considered relevant. However, you will be more able to develop the power to steer that kind of knowledge to your own advantage only after you have set within you a strong foundation for it. You may no longer need to struggle to make practical information work, but you may rather be able to positively apply the techniques at your own pace…. and that is when you become a super selling machine! (…I just had to say that).

It was time for a change

My focus soon expanded. The spotlight was no longer exclusively placed on my husband and his approach, but with help from peers and other professionals in the field, I was able to collect extraordinary feedback. I had a chance to interact with people from different sales areas and backgrounds. I witnessed a wider variety of verbal and non-verbal behaviors, better yet, I was able to ask questions, and in the process, I learned more about each person's individual approach, and results.

Now, it is not my intention to sound irrational, but what I was able to figure out was so disturbingly simple, yet outrageously overlooked (stay with me please): **Those with a *negative* mentality, never accomplished *positive* results.** The way I just introduced my point, should be an indication of how shocked I was that part of the answer had been so simple all along, yet an overwhelming number of individuals in this profession opt for a negative mentality and still wonder why their expectations are not easily met. It seems as if it all comes down to a simple equation:

PM + PA = IR (Positive Mentality + Positive Attitude = Improved Results)

So, if it is supposed to be that simple, why isn't it entirely *natural* for everyone? Why don't we all automatically function based on such a concept? The answer may reside in our minds, where the notion may constantly face an internal challenge, running the risk of being discarded as unnecessary, obvious, or worse yet, a waste of time; and it all could easily occur due to lack of awareness.

By drawing an invisible line down the middle to compare stagnant results with outcomes that involve *success* and a *positive flow* of experiences, we should easily conclude that it might not be such a waste of time after all. On the contrary, by allotting time each day to improving our mindset, and learning a fresh approach to match that new frame of mind, we may not only be able to perform better, but we may also be able to remain sane and happy in the process.

Working from the inside could mean a shift in the perception that selling is supposed to be *hard*, and in exchange, sales may become a skill that you could soon perform with more *passion*, and less stress. (Yes, you read right…passion!).

Now back to me.

I always thought I was doing things right. I had drive, and I was always determined to meet my goals; but what I was truly faced with… was a daily dose of struggle. Time, effort, and money spent on books were obviously not making much difference. On the other hand, it so happened, that being around other sales professionals did.

While spending time with colleges and other salespeople from different fields and backgrounds, I was able to observe two different types of individual. Starting with the kind who is able to tap into his/ her internal abilities, able to exceed sales expectations, break records, and remain a top producer in the process.

I noticed something special while interacting with each one of them. They were all full of energy and positivity. I was amazed at the vibe I was getting. They seemed relaxed. It looked as if they were not even trying.

Their view on sales was similar to a 'go with the flow' approach. I also noticed that the type of clients they encountered allowed for a higher earning potential; meaning their prospects showed a tendency to request higher-priced products, generating top commissions... And if by now, you are wondering... yes, I did double check, and none of them were related to the vice president of their company. A majority of call centers and other businesses appeared to have a system designed to route calls based on a first come, first served basis status. Was it luck then?

I was definitely willing to consider it all random fortune, until I realized that what was taking place was more than an occurrence. It was rather a constant stream of positive sales events. At some point, I concluded that instead of luck, these individuals were truly *creating* their day!

I also witnessed the opposite kind of sales professionals. I'm referring to the type that frequently complained, and in his own words, described sales as a *"never-ending battle."* Within this group, there was a common agreement that competition is supposed to be a "vital element of the sales process..." One with the primary purpose of ensuring their "survival."

It all seemed harmless, until I noticed that some of the attitude and negativity they expressed while off duty, somehow reflected while on the job. It wasn't my initial mission to gauge their level of success, but by observing the discrepancy in results and production between one type and the other, I started to see a relevance that exceeded any of my original expectations.

This well-stated contrast somehow established the possible existence of two different approaches—one of them with the potential to attract a positive flow of sales experiences; and another one in which struggle was the continual result.

I personally decided it was time for a change. Either I stayed behind struggling with my own routine, or move on to the one process that could help me achieve my goals more effectively. At that point, I was certain that an alternative might exist.

I would eventually get my job back. My boss was gracious enough to write it all off as a moment of insanity, but I now cherish the time I spent away, when I was able to pause, breathe, and get myself back together. Too bad Republicans and Democrats have not so far. They may need a bit more time.

SKY IS THE LIMIT

*The mind is the limit. As long as the mind can envision
the fact that you can do something, you can do it, as long
as you really believe 100 percent.*
—David Hockney

I don't remember knowing much about God during my childhood.
What I do remember is that whenever I wanted something special to
happen, or to land on my hands, like a toy or my parents taking me
to my favorite pizza place, I would look high into the sky and ask.
Truthfully, I don't know if I was gazing up into the sky expecting to
communicate my desires to God, or just hoping for a shooting star to
show up so that I could place my wish, but from an early age, I saw a
correlation between *the sky* and the act of asking or *hoping* for things
to improve.

My parents, including my godfather, always made every effort to
provide me with the best education possible. At eleven years old, I was
placed in a prestigious school, renown for teaching kids English as a
second language. I was very fortunate.

One day in class, while on the topic of idioms, I learned the expression, *the sky is the limit.* The phrase and its connotation struck me as somewhat fascinating, and at that very young age, it seemed as if I had found my motto. I was a kid, though, so instead I kept repeating, *"Sky's the limit,"* with certain cockiness, and mostly when I was surrounded by people… just to show off my English skills. I would sometimes test my family and friends, and randomly ask (in English), *"Do you know what it means?"*

On almost every occasion, I got looks of pride, and amazement, but somehow I think I overdid it. Soon everybody thought I was being rather annoying (especially while I was chewing gum), and I was asked to shut up, and keep it to myself.

The sky is the limit is an expression commonly used to remind us that it is possible to transcend boundaries we may be setting within ourselves. It reminds us to be positive and optimistic about the possibilities, and all that we can achieve. The expression, eventually took on a different meaning when, once more I very arrogantly tried to explain the expression to one of my little friends in the neighborhood. After I finished my explanation, he looked at me, much perplexed, and following the long pause it took for him to grasp what I had just said, he responded, (in Spanish, off course) *"I didn't know the sky had any limits."*

A truly creative person rids him or herself of all self-imposed limitations.
—Gerald Jampolsky

Sadly, there are companies in America that do cap and place a certain limit on the employee's level of production. In that case, the title of this book may not mean much to those in that situation. And while I do hope that those specific businesses change such policies at some point, I also hope that you are part of the greater number of workers whose companies encourage and expect higher productivity from their employees, giving you, off course, greater chances to earn more. If that is the case (…or not) then, stick around, I got news for you!

There are many reasons why the expression, *The sky is the limit* can be fitting for any person working in the profession; starting with the fact that regardless of the number of superiors running the company, in sales, you are the one person in charge! Yes, there are certain levels of performance and expectations; but in the end, the size of the paycheck, and the success in the career is ultimately up to us and to our ability to perform (Sell! Sell! Sell!). While other professions are strongly driven by timetables, curriculums, strict programming, scrutiny, and even micro managing, those in sales are more likely to experience a little more 'elbowroom.' But it is precisely in the 'size of the paycheck' part that the concept applies best.

With a few exemptions, sales, is a job with very attractive and *unlimited* earning potential. In other words, right at your fingertips, are all the chances needed to meet your personal financial goals. So, what is stopping you from doubling or even tripling your production? Who is putting a ceiling on your earnings?

The answer to all those questions lies in the simple but profound process of the way you *think*. Yes, the key is in your mind. It is sad to say that the only person putting a ceiling on your own income is YOU. There is no other person or reason to blame. It is neither the situation of the country, nor the company you work for. It is not your choice of computer, and believe me, it is definitely not the moon.

By aligning the right mentality, along with the right attitude, just as a common battery must be aligned to its proper pole, it could be possible to convert feelings of struggle and stress into feelings of flow and calm. You could then be on our way to creating the so-called *energy source* that could make it all work more smoothly; one that could help you master all the challenges keeping you from fulfilling your maximum earning potential. Furthermore, new developments possible by following the proper sales process may include a new outlook on the profession, an improvement on the relationship with peers and superiors, and a newfound joy while interacting with customers.

I am neither a psychologist, nor a financial advisor. I do not know many complicated terms, and I am not here to crunch the numbers for you. What I am willing to do is to further express what works for me and for many of the most successful people in the field (even when sometimes they don't even know it).

It is my theory that a majority of us have been conditioned to follow a process that stands on the *negative* side of the spectrum. I would like to take this opportunity to remind you that there is definitely a *positive* side to sales. If you also believe it is time for a change, then, pause, breathe…and get ready for it. Let this book be your tool of inspiration to get started now.

CHAPTER ONE

The Creative and Competitive Processes

It is safe to say times are changing. Selling is an activity no longer limited to the usual phone-based or face-to face interaction. As much as I would like to express that the possibilities are endless for us in the profession, it is relevant to point out that they are as endless for the customer as well.

All it takes is the touch of a button. Regardless of your line of business or sales background, there is a common denominator that unites us all, and that is *technology*. The real question is what would set us apart.

Cell phone applications and mobile devices such as BlackBerry's, iPads, iPhones have not only broken barriers, but they have also changed the game. The customer now has endless and constant access to offers, promotions, and information. Any company or individual can easily reach your potential client at any moment via e-mail and web links. Marketing now is as simple as logging into a Facebook or Tweeter account; and for android phone users, the world of unlimited data is available at their fingertips as fast as they can aim for a barcode. Now more than ever the methods you use to not only reach your clients, but to keep their business as well, are crucial.

I will now present to you the two different processes that could make the difference. No longer on a search, I am able to explain the distinction between one approach and the other.

As you will soon notice, by the simple act of working within one of the processes you could automatically provide your customer with invaluable service. The process is set upon the premise of building and maintaining trust. It is, the one process that may allow you to reach your goals in a more balanced manner; creating a path that could lead to more freedom, calm, and security; transforming the way you think about sales; and ultimately influencing outcomes in a more positive way.

The alternate process, on the other hand, could seem to be the easiest and most comfortable approach on the surface. It is even considered as the one that requires the least amount of effort; and that could be just an illusion, since the results usually involve disappointment and setbacks.

I am referring to the *Creative* and the *Competitive* processes—two very different approaches, standing at opposite ends of the spectrum. One of them is based in *fear*, while the other one is based in *faith*. One provokes *reaction*…the opposite, *creation*. While it is essential to be familiar with the way each of these two processes work, it is equally important to identify which one you are currently applying to your daily routine.

Switching from one process to the other is very easy—easier than we realize, and precisely the reason why it is essential to be aware and conscious at every level. In other words, it is time we push the cruise control button off, and become more involved with our own everyday acts and decisions.

THE COMPETITIVE PROCESS

*A creative man is motivated by the desire to
achieve, not by the desire to beat others*
—Ayn Rand

Do you watch sporting events? Olympics, Masters, Tournaments? If yes, then most likely you have seen individuals at their highest level of competitiveness. You have seen them push harder, pull longer, and fight to the end. You have seen them bleed, sweat, and even cry.

In sports, the challenger's next move is a *reaction* greatly based on the competitor's move; and winning or losing is determined upon *judging*, or by the *comparison* of the final scores. This is all exciting to see, especially in a boxing ring, a car race, and even in a chess game. I am not sure though, that the same pattern should be applied in our place of work. Sadly, in sales this is a very common model. Sports are *physical*. Reaction, comparison of scores, and going after the competition should be part of it all; but basing our personal or business lives on such external factors, could soon make us feel as if we just got lost in the game.

Regardless of whether it is applied to win tournaments, advancing in our careers, or for purposes of our personal lives, the Competitive will always be based on the same standards and principles. This approach is all about the reaction to external situations processed by the individual as a threat. A threat based on a perception that could develop into *anxiety* and *fear*. Several examples of the types of fear that the person could experience include fear of failure, fear of being left behind, fear of scarcity, and fear of rejection…And in sales, they all apply.

Some of that fear could at times be considered helpful and even necessary. It could easily be viewed as the basis for market innovation and for the expansion of products and services. Picture for example, the progress in the area of electronics and software. By the invention of one item, a multinational business corporation could have left their competitors in the dark ages (I am not going to mention any names… Apple). It is by a dose of the fear that drives the Competitive process that other major companies in the market refuse to *stay behind*, *fail*, or *lose* their relevant place in the industry, and now you and I are able to enjoy a variety of products similar to the original version, and at even better prices. Love it!

But as much as I do understand that individuals and corporations have long implemented competitive standards and that those practices can be partly credited with their 'success,' I remind you that the information found here is strictly designed to highlight the advantages and disadvantages of each process from an emotional level. It is done with the purpose to draw attention as to how each approach can have an impact in the individual's attitude, performance, habits, thinking and indeed, in the quality of his/her results.

Companies are going to do whatever they believe is best to encourage production. The question is what are YOU going to do to keep your sanity?

Being involved in all the dynamics at work can be fun and exciting. Whether it is a contest, a match, or a challenge, your participation should not be a considered a problem; it is actually the approach we take that makes the difference. Those types of activities are known to stimulate the individual, and in some cases, they can even be encouraging and motivating, since they promote the desire in the individual to stretch to match or exceed coworkers' scores. Yet, I encourage you to remember at all times, that it is not about the game…it is all about the strategy.

Pick up a dictionary...any dictionary, and search for the word *Competition*. Most likely, you will encounter at least one or two of the following words associated with the term: *rivalry, contention, tug of war, and aggression*. Some more positive definitions of the term like, *spirited, gung ho, and 'ready for action'* may come up. Based on that contrast, I am not surprised that many of us in the field choose competing as the most useful approach based on the notion that it is a 'good enough' combination that somehow works, and it gets the job done. That is how many of us are getting by...it seems that we are conforming to 'good enough.'

A great number of salespeople would credit their success to their competitive drive. Competition to them feels like a rush that compels them to push harder and work tirelessly. In sales, competition can be considered at times a given; and a feature that has developed into an integral part of the job description. However, the question arises...is competition the healthy pathway to our targets?

By daily living the competitive habit at work, we tend to generate within ourselves the feeling that enough is never enough. We are driven by a need to be better than somebody else, a struggle to have better numbers on the board, and a constant quest to get more recognition from superiors and managers, just to mention a few. This conditioning could make it harder for the individual to achieve a personal feeling of accomplishment or satisfaction, and that could become one of the major risk factor for the levels of stress known to plague workers today.

People can be easily drawn into competition much the same way many become addicted to sugar-based products, including candies and drinks. The products promise that coveted pick-me-up, and of course their sweet taste, but in the end, the effects and results of working within the Competitive could be eerily similar: an initial rush, destined to end up in a crash.

It is under this process that many are encouraged to feel that it is necessary to go to work prepared for battle; one in which the main strategy includes tactics for 'beating' numbers; those of outside competitors, as well as those from peers within the organization. We are transforming our workplace into a battlefield. Do you know what happens when we head to work every day prepared for war? Well, we make war..., sometimes on ourselves!

At the end of the day, even after meeting all sales expectations, it is important to ask ourselves if it was all worth it. I am talking about the stress, tension, desperation, and even at some point, that 'burned-out' feeling.

NIOSH (National Institute for Occupational Safety and Health) is a federal agency responsible for conducting studies for the prevention of work-related injuries (Niosh.com). Some of their findings report that job stress is believed to increase the risk for muscle disorders and other illnesses that could be at fault for excessive health care utilization. Science Daily (Sciencedaily.com) is an award-winning site dedicated to the latest research news. According to two separate reports published in their website, scientists at The University of Western Ontario have discovered the link between stress, anxiety and depression (Apr.19, 2010). Their latest article reports that the same group of scientists has found the first direct evidence confirming a link between stress and heart attacks (Sept 4, 2010).

It is commonly understood that people with known levels of excessive stress could experience loss of appetite, restless sleep, and a complete sense of exhaustion. Other known health risks associated with stress include, depression, migraine headaches, skin problems...and now, according to Bob Harper, the trainer for the hit television show, The Biggest Loser, stress can even make us fat (Based on his new book, *Are You Ready?*).

It does not stop there. The tension seems to reflect back into one's personal life. It seems that despite the technological advances of our times, a switch to turn off all the after-work stress is still long way from invention. In the meantime, a great number of people will most likely experience the consequences of stress after leaving work and its ripple effects in our personal lives; affecting the way we interact with those, we love.

So, why is stress so predominant in our line of work…or in any other profession for that matter?

See Jason's case, for example. He remained a top producer in his company for quite some time, until realizing that his numbers and income were nowhere close to years past. What affected him most, he says, was noticing all the fresh, new sales staff coming into the organization, "pulling up higher numbers." His wife started to notice how he was becoming irritable and short-tempered. Jason later began expressing to her, his concerns about how he pulled ten to twelve hour shifts trying to exceed sales expectations; and how no matter how hard he tried he was still not able to figure out how to perform at the same level that placed others on top.

It seemed to me that Jason was having somewhat of a breakdown himself. It is clear, based on his own reports, that he was placing more attention on other people rather than on himself. He never said he did not meet sales goals or expectations; it seems, instead, that he was struggling to *exceed* other's. His case can ultimately teach us that we lose our power when we focus on others; and it reminds us of the relevance of finding a process that give us the ability to keep the power within us.

Truth is, consciously or unconsciously, most of us have been conditioned to be competitive. Schools ignite the competitive spirit through sports, scores, and grades. Friends encourage one another to be competitive through games and bets. Society rewards competition with scholarships, and trophies…and the list goes on.

For those growing up with brothers and sisters, who doesn't remember at least a point in life when our parents thought it would be a great idea to compare our achievements… or lack of them…with our siblings? Some parents go as far as to say, *"You are nothing like him/her." "Or why can't you be more like your sister (or brother)?"*

I would not be surprised if some of you felt a need to compete for your parents' attention from an early age, by struggling to meet specific expectations, based on their level of satisfaction of your own brothers and sisters.

I think educators should know better, but I still clearly remember the pressure not to fall behind my classmates' performance in order to stay in the good graces of some of my favorite teachers. Nowadays, there are even websites set up with the sole purpose of letting parents compare their kids' test scores with their peers nationwide (e.g., GreatSchools. net). As if, there is not enough pressure already at home, let alone competing with the whole country.

It is not my intention to criticize any of the methods used to help our kids succeed, given that I am neither a parent nor an educator myself. It is also not the purpose of this book to underestimate the importance of competition, since I do recognize its overall importance, for the economy and the consumers as well.

My intent is solely directed toward the personal *well-being*—a word that many dictionaries describe as *the state of being healthy, happy, or prosperous.* It is my intention to highlight the importance of an approach that could reduce the well-known effects of stress associated with the profession, while increasing profits and improving results.

The Encyclopædia Britannica has many variations and references for words related to *competition*, but this one is their main and first option to describe the term:

… Within a species, either all members obtain part of a necessary resource such as food or space, or some individuals obtain enough for their needs while other members, cut off from the resource, die or are forced to inhabit a less suitable or marginal area. Young members of a population are most often adversely affected.

The following is the description of the word Competition according to the Merriam-Webster Dictionary:

1: The act or process of, competing, rivalry: The effort of two or more parties acting independently to secure the business of a third party by offering the most favorable terms (b) active demand by two or more organisms or kinds of organisms for some environmental resource in short supply 2: A contest between rivals.

Note how both definitions involve organisms, species, and the environment. The word seems to be strongly associated to *nature* in general. It is time we realize that competition may well be a trait that we are born with, rather than one acquired exclusively to deal with daily demands; and based on the definitions, it may not be a negative one after all, since it compels us to *'survive.'* Both definitions however, also involve the concepts of *limited supply* (resources), *rivalry, and adversity*, so based on that, the question arises: …Is it a competitive approach what is dragging us down to a path where stress at work becomes a *natural* element of our everyday life?

Well, who knows best about species, organism, and natural selection than *Charles Darwin* himself? He wrote the book about it, after all. Maybe he can provide the answer to that question. His now most famous quote reads,

It is not the strongest of the species that survives, nor the most intelligent that survives. It is the one that is most adaptable to change.
—Charles Darwin

It is fitting to say that theories about evolution and those similar are in opposition to the Creative concept. I remind you that this book is committed to highlighting the parallel existence of opposite course of actions, points of views or processes. (See Appendix A for more information). Even so, Mr. Darwin himself clearly supports the concept of the Creative process as being the most effective route.

His comment reassures us that it is not about being *stronger, faster, wittier* or even working *harder* or more tirelessly (if we put it in a work-related context). It is about being the least resistant to change, which is one of the applications found while working within creative standards. So, allow me introduce you to the Creative.

THE CREATIVE PROCESS

Every human has four endowments- self-awareness, conscience, independent will and creative imagination. These give us the ultimate human freedom. The power to choose, to respond, to change.
—Stephen Covey

Dr. Stephen R. Covey (Best-selling author) is one of the many influential and successful people who remind us through their words that being creative is innate within our human nature; much the same way I previously expressed how being competitive is a natural trait that we all may be born with as well. *Self-awareness; conscience; independent will; the power to choose, respond and change*—they will all make more sense as you venture into this process. A process that I am almost certain, you have heard about before.

The Creative process is the lifeline for many professionals and individuals regardless of their craft or business field. It is the one undeniable factor linked to the success of an extensive list of careers and occupations. Designers, architects, and inventors cannot perform without it. Advertisers and marketing teams thrive on it; and it is undoubtedly essential for performers, writers, and artists as well. If Darwin's words hold any truth, then being creative is what truly guarantees our *survival*, since it is under this process that humans *"have the power to be responsive to change."*

Being creative allows us to grow, expand and develop. It allows us to generate ideas and solutions to improve our lives. Can you imagine us, as a race, in a world in which we were not creative? In the best-case scenario, it is possible that we would simply live in caves.

Creation starts in our mind. Everything in existence today began with a thought, with just a simple idea.

Comparing sales with some of the most popular occupations that come to mind, we quickly understand that our approach to the Creative, as a course of action, must be different. We are not producing physical merchandise like the fashion designer (shoes, clothes, etc.). Our final product is not an artifact such as the latest toy or the next 'hot' item. It is not something that people can look at repeatedly, like a nationwide TV ad or the most popular magazine in the country.

Our final product is in *the ability* to move thousands of products that produce profits. Our value is established by our demonstrated *skill* to generate those profits; and our major goal is *attracting* the right prospects. By applying simple, but powerful *changes* in attitude and mentality, the Creative process is there to help you achieve just that.

Several key items make this process possible and successful:

o   By nature, people are attracted to others who exude confidence and knowledge.

o   They positively respond to people who project a spirit of progress and growth.

o   They would not overlook an opportunity to interact with people who could potentially improve their lives.

o   In addition, the more people you are ready to serve, the higher your earning potential.

The major and most important key, however, will become clear, after realizing that amazing things happen when we place ourselves on a path of least resistance – that is when we allow great things to flow. Our best ideas are born when we least struggle. This is accomplished with a mind free from doubt and while following a routine that minimizes the major stress factors that plague workers today.

Using just a few words, the online Merriam-Webster dictionary could not explain the process any better—*Creative: Marked by the ability and power to create.* And this is the definition of the verb *create*, according to the same dictionary: *(a) To bring into existence <God created the heaven and the earth— Genesis 1:1. (b) To produce or bring about by a course of action or behavior.*

It is clear, based on that definition that the Creative involves power. How else do you bring into existence what is not yet a reality? The role of that power in the process is signified by the *abilities* that every one of us posses. Abilities that when properly applied can enhance our level of performance. Some examples include passion, confidence, determination, knowledge, leadership, empathy, resistance, awareness, persuasion, and the most fundamental ingredient…faith. Properly applied, the process works, and it is bound to bring increased productivity, and genuine good results.

Synonyms of the word creative include, *visionary, clever, gifted, innovative, formative, original, inspired, ingenious,* and even *cool.* Now, that sounds more like it!

WHAT IS THE DIFFERENCE?

"The way of the Creative works through change and transformation, so that each thing receives its true nature and destiny and comes into permanent accord with the Great Harmony: this is what furthers and what perseveres"—Alexander Pope (1688-1744)

Whether you are now working within the Competitive or the Creative Process, there is no doubt that meeting your goals is achievable. The difference between using one process and the other, however, is in how *hard or uncomplicated* you would like it to be.

"God gave us free will" is an expression used to remind us that all throughout the different kinds of situations we face on a day-to-day basis, we retain our power to make decisions; and the way we act or react is ultimately up to us.

Considering the number of salespeople who are extremely successful in their profession, and the potentially even greater number of those who are not, we should conclude that our occupation is not exempt from that principle of choice. So what are our options? The answer may lie within the Creative and Competitive processes. This section elaborates in the elements that differentiate one process from the other.

The Competitive Process: The reason why fear is the prime emotion in this process is that the Competitive, as a course of action, is born from insecurities. Lack of confidence can easily drive the individual to get into competitive gear. The person could automatically feel the need to 'keep watch' on his neighbor in order to gauge his own level of success. That same insecurity will keep the individual *looking to the right and to the left* to observe somebody else's achievements and performance, rather than focusing on himself, and as a result, that person could find himself too busy *looking back* (comparing and judging) that he would most likely forget to look ahead; therefore planning, vision, and expectation, are values 'lost in the process.'

With a competitive mind, the salesperson is set on the idea that there is a limited amount of resources, therefore, the will to *'get what belongs to me before somebody else does'*…is running in high gear. The main message is that 'there is not enough to go around.' This limiting thought process could force the individual to choose a more aggressive approach. The first clue telling you that this is happening unconsciously is when the salesperson rationalizes the act of being *insistent* and *aggressive* as being 'essential' to getting the sale, and describes him/herself as being a 'go-getter' thinking that it is the most effective approach. In this process, cooperation and teamwork may be possible, but in essence, not considered a priority.

The Creative Process: Passion, conviction, hope, assurance, belief, and trust, are all associated with the word *faith*. If there is ever a quality able to help you succeed, and prosper, it is on that short list; but there is an actual reason why faith is a fundamental value in the process. For starters, *Creative*, implies inspiration and vision, but mostly, it derives from the word creation. *Creation* is about bringing forth events, results, and products that did not previously exist; and the 'substance' that could make it all happen…well, that would be *faith*.

The interesting thing about it is that faith only looks toward one direction…*forward*. It does not get busy with the past, and the present is just the stepping-stone for what is ahead—And that is the reason why visionaries and people that are bound to make a difference in the world fully rely on the Creative process as their source for inspiration, ideas, vision, and motivation. What better example than *Thomas Edison* himself—the man credited with the invention of the light bulb, and off course, keeping in line with the topic of energy sources.

According to an article found in the Smithsonian Institute website (www.si.edu), Thomas Edison developed a practical light bulb toward the end of 1879. In 1880, he designed the first version to have all the essential features of a modern light bulb. That invention however, did not happen overnight. According to the Institute, Thomas Edison tried *hundreds of times* to make filaments that would glow and not burn up. (www.invention.smithsonian.org). Yes, hundreds of times…in fact, legend has it that Thomas Edison tried and failed 2,000 times, while others speculate that he could have actually tried as many as 9,999 times before finding success. All based on his own now famous words.

"I never failed once. It just happened to be a 2000- step process."
—Thomas Edison

"Young man, why would I feel like a failure? And why would I ever give up? I now know definitively over 9,000 ways that an electric light bulb will not work. Success is almost in my grasp."
—Thomas Edison.

…And if you thought that on any given day, maybe while on his eight-hundredth attempt, Edison at some point got concerned about the aspect of his *present* situation, think again! According to his own words, Edison was only looking toward one direction…*forward!*

*"If I find 10,000 ways something won't work, I haven't failed.
I am not discouraged, because every wrong attempt discarded*

*is another **step forward**. Just because something doesn't do what you planned it to do doesn't mean it's useless."*
—Thomas Edison

*"Be courageous. I have seen many depressions in business. Always America has emerged from these stronger and more prosperous. Be brave as your fathers before you. **Have faith! Go forward!***"
—Thomas A. Edison

When you can create, there is no need to set limits. There is abundance and plenty of resources in the Creative process. The mind is creative by nature. Our task is to make the connection, and place our thoughts and attitudes in harmony with it. While working in the Creative process your thoughts are expansive. The mind is free to expect the next customer. The last call was not your last, and more prospects are waiting to do business with you. In other words, you are working under the mindset of increase. In this process, you are also working with a mind free from doubt and insecurities; therefore, when properly performed, worry, anxiety, stress, and fear are not part of the process, or they will at least be present at their 'lowest degree.'

"Shoot for the moon and even if you miss you will still be among the stars" —Les Brown

---

The sky is the limit is an expression designed to remind us about the possibilities. Personally, it reminds me to look up. What does it mean to you? Have you shot for the stars yet? Have you ever wondered how far you can go? The Creative Process is not a new concept in any way. For decades, millionaires and great minds have been trying to deliver the message…I think it is time we listen.

Switching from the Competitive to the Creative process involves a shift in mentality. For some, this could be effortless, while others may need more time. That is why I will always remind you to keep *aware* and *conscious* at all levels. That is my request for you to place focus on how you think (mind) and how you act (attitude).

Below is an example of how those two main aspects in the process— mind and attitude, align during your basic approach:

Competitive Standards: Under this process you could frequently find yourself more concerned with meeting sales quotas and *'beating your competitor's numbers,'* rather than anything else. You could then start viewing the customer as someone you can benefit from, rather than someone *you* could benefit with your expertise and assistance. The customer then becomes your 'resource' to gaining a new sales transaction that would give you a 'lead' or 'advantage.'

The high stakes placed on that sole transaction could set in motion a chain reaction of events that may seem 'normal' and at times even 'expected.' Starting with the fact that the contemplation of failure is strong enough to heighten what we know as the *fear of rejection*. It is then that you might 'cling' to the customer, as if that prospect was the last and only one. Ultimately, your tone of voice, and even your attitude may expose your irritability and desperation. Customers are at times able to pick up these vibes, and as a result, you have greatly reduced your chances of closing the sale.

On the other hand, individuals working within *creative standards* aim for a more positive attitude that automatically reflects on the quality of service. In this process, it is understood that the primary task is caring for your customer's needs first, which is precisely what will turn a potential transaction into a relationship. That could set in motion a series of positive responses that are bound to create a sense of trust-—priceless in any business dealings.

By means of your behavior, approach, and attitude, you have set yourself apart, and that could be a key factor for not only sales increase and customer retention, but also, repeat business, and referrals. There is no doubt that when the customer has a high-quality experience, everybody wins.

As a side note…by now, you might have noticed I have used the preposition *under* when referring to working within the standards of each process. The Competitive and the Creative Processes demand different mindsets and approaches to the tasks of sales. The actual advantages…or disadvantages, for that matter, of each process are not only in their execution, per se, but in their influence. It is precisely like saying, *working under the influence…* acknowledging the need for concentration, and experiencing the effect on your acts and decisions.

Moving on, those working under the Creative Process know that the more people they serve, the higher their earning potential. Not only that, but by servicing and being open to other people's needs they can easily create within themselves a gratifying feeling of accomplishment, and a sense of purpose…and that's not a bad reason to go to work.

Awareness During Each Process

by now you may be able to recognize which process you choose to follow based on your daily approach (mind and attitude); but if you still feel that you need assistance identifying where you stand, below is a list that compares just a few of the most noticeable feelings and actions under each process:

Individuals under the Creative Process	Individuals under the Competitive Process
They are *grateful* for their jobs	They tend to *complain* about their jobs
They *serve* the individual	They resort to *pressure* and demands
They *believe* in the value of their product	They *criticize* their product
Welcome the interaction with prospects	They *dread* meeting with customers
They are *upbeat and full of energy*	They show *lack* of interest and confidence
Eager to learn/Open to new information	*Frustrated* about changes and updates
Genuinely happy about others' success	*Envious* and jealous of others' success
Always *expecting* a *positive* outcome	They remain *fearful of rejection*

The characteristics of some of the behaviors mentioned in the list provide clues to recognizing whether we are on the right path or just running around in circles. Please take a second look at it, and notice how each process provides a certain kind of *feelings and actions* that follow:

In the list related to the Competitive, feelings of limitation, fear, anger, stress, frustration, and envy were noticeable. The Creative process, however, brought out feelings of freedom, passion, positivity, expectation, and flow.

I kept a brief handwritten list of pros and cons pinned to my desk at all times to remind me of the potential results I should expect by working within each process. I actually called it, the *"Pros and Comps List,"* because I placed the positives where they belong (pros), to indicate the results that fall under the Creative; and I called the negatives *comps* instead, to signify that they fall under the **Comp**etitive.

PROS	COMPS
I REMAIN **PROFESSIONAL**	I CHOOSE TO **COMPETE**
I ATTRACT MORE **PROSPECTS**	I PROCEED TO **COMPARE**
I NCREASE MY **PROFITS**	I AM SURE TO **COMPLAIN**

That list is brief, but effective. It starts with a *choice* down to the *results*. The first line is precisely an example of the choice any of us can make, *consciously* or *unconsciously*. The second line points out the *influence*, which indicates either the *benefit* or the *reaction* that the decision might cause; and the last sentence reveals the *results*. Once you become aware of the way each process works and the possible benefits or reactions, you could make your own list. Let's review it one more time:

PROS: Using the Creative approach means working from the inside. Choosing the proper course of action will place you in a state of flow. Rushing your customer to make a decision, or raising your voice in frustration is not necessary. You *remain more* **pro**fessional and in control…a major key to *attracting and welcoming* more **pro**spects, repeat business, and referrals. Increased **pro**fits, you ask? Well, again that is just the result.

You want your customer to get the unmistakable feeling that he is dealing with someone who has his best interest at heart. Your prospect can sense the overall pleasant expressions, the kinder tone of voice, and the sincere smile. You, on the other hand, can see in this person the appreciation and confidence in your services, which translate into more information, openness, and even one or two stories from the customer. This mutual exchange sets a [connection] that will inadvertently give you an edge over the competition.

CONS (COMPS): Individuals working under the **Comp**etitive Process tend to focus on external conditions to determine their next step, which will be no more than a reaction to the circumstances that surround them, or to what they perceive. That is the reason why **comp**aring, is inevitable, and almost a must.

The list that belongs to the Competitive approach would most likely describe the individual that sees the need to know where he/she stands in comparison to coworker's numbers, position, timing, and more. As I have previously mentioned, this can be exhilarating and even fun at times. The problem, though, is that somebody else is always going to be faster, stronger, better, more charismatic, have higher numbers and, well…you get it. This could be the start of a long struggle.

Complaining and becoming frustrated are only part of the deal, and a very predictable outcome. The average age for retirement is sixty-two years old. Can you imagine the damage produced by the slow and gradual accumulation of stress? I personally do not think is worth it…would you?

TO GET STARTED

---

*"If you want to develop your **creativity**, establish regular work habits. Allow time for the incubation of ideas, and adhere to your individual rhythm. Violations of this rhythm can retard your creative efficiency"* —Eugene Raudsepp

---

I am not offering you a fast solution. What I am offering, is the combination of new and traditional techniques introduced in an uplifting and refreshing manner. The purpose is to positively transform your approach, and the outcome of your workday.

The Merriam-Webster dictionary, gives the word *process* the following descriptions:

(a) A natural phenomenon marked by gradual changes that lead toward a particular result. (b) A systematic series of actions or operations directed to some end.

Awareness will be the first ability required to start the process, but having self-awareness rooted deep within our being as one of our most innate qualities, is not a guarantee that we are using it as one of our most powerful abilities. Self-awareness is the one skill that can help us identify the traits and values that make us who we are; with it, we are able to perceive aspects of our personality, like our inclinations, strengths, weaknesses, and tendencies. Blame it on the atmosphere of our social climate, or maybe on our busy-day lives, but nowadays we seem more preoccupied with what is happening around us than within us. Nowadays, it is easier to describe more and more people as being self-disengaged rather than being self-aware.

And with that in mind, consider the chapters that follow as your user's guide. Your non-sense 'how- to' manual designed to gradually steer you into the Creative Process.

CHAPTER TWO

Loving What You Do

Passion is in all great searches and is necessary to all creative endeavors.
—W. Eugene Smith

Passion is fundamental for all endeavors in life...or at least for those in which you want to be successful. Without passion and desire, there is no motivation, no inspiration, no enthusiasm, no desire, and no interest. You are missing the essential feelings associated with taking action in a positive way. You run the risk of getting into a rut. Without passion, you are setting yourself up for failure.

Proof that passion is a vital feature of any career or occupation is found in some of the greatest artists and performers that have shaped our culture. If given the opportunity, well-known figures like Tiger Woods, Taylor Swift, and Tyler Perry will be quick to credit their love for what they do and passion for their careers as the main factor to achieving their phenomenal success, and the riches they now enjoy.

The Biography Channel is packed with documentaries based on some of the most influential people in history; and while the accounts may vary, it is actually very common to find the inspirational stories of those who started with barely anything, just with the desire and determination to be the best in their field. It would seem as if fame and fortune just happened to follow.

Granted, our profession is nowhere as glitzy and high profile as theirs, but that is no reason or excuse for us not to be as proud and passionate about ours.

During the past ten years of my career in sales, I have had the opportunity to experience firsthand all types of individuals, and their attitudes toward the occupation. I present to you a few of those types in an attempt to bring to your attention some of the most common cases. I will then let you decide if you have personally met or encountered any of them:

The Energy Sucker (The type that drains your positive energy)— Let's say you arrive fresh in the morning, ready to start your day. You rush into the elevator before the door closes. Somebody was nice enough to hold it for you. To avoid the awkward silence, you asked what you thought was a simple question, "How are you?"—Just three words, right?

The answer will obviously vary, but if you are talking to the Energy Sucker type, you will most likely hear expressions that include, *"Well, what do you expect? It is Monday," "I would prefer to be at home sleeping!"* and the now famous…*"I wish I had won the lottery over the weekend."* This person is not as 'pumped up' as you are to start your day, and it is their lack of purpose and positive energy that will take yours away, ultimately bringing you down to their level of frustration…beware!

The Negative Magnet (The type that attracts negative experiences)— Two words of advice for you…run away! There is no positive experience from this individual's point of view, and he tends to be very vocal about it. Unfortunately, negativity is more infectious than the common cold, and as innocent as it may seem, the negativity that flows out tends to turn around in the shape of negative experiences, and my guess is that you may not want to be anywhere near its path while on the way back. This type will be easy to spot…Most likely, once or twice you have seen those wearing casts or crutches.

The Happy-Go-Lucky (The type that couldn't care less)—This is the 'cool guy' in the office. This title belongs to the individual you frequently see wandering around, sometimes just chatting and joking. A few minutes with him and you will be certain to hear expressions that include the popular, *"Let's see how the day goes, dude."* But in essence, this is really the 'luckiest' type of all. It is common to hear him say, *"I got another huge sale!"* and it always makes you wonder how in the heck that happens?!

People usually attribute it to beginners' luck; but the actual reason would be that this one is the type that almost got it. Yes, you heard right. They almost got the concept of flow. One of the reasons why they completely *do not* is their lack of *passion*. This type is very easy to recognize since they usually think the 'extra mile' is a new energy drink.

The Good is Never Enough (The type that is always dissatisfied)— This one is the type who frequently places the customer in an undeserving and unflattering light. They are easy to recognize, since it is customary for them to complain about the client, "He was too slow," or, "She was talking too fast." At some point you marvel at their passion to tell the story about how the customer asked the most obvious questions three or four times.

What is truly amazing is that this type sticks to their ways even after the customer proved to be a genuine buyer. Their trait is to volunteer their recent 'stories' even when you are not asking.

...And the list will go on. Feel free to add any other type of characters you may encounter. Before moving on, though, let me point out that if any of the types of individuals previously described were truly passionate about their occupation, they would share a different outlook, a different way to face situations, and a different demeanor. There is not a chance that they could feel negative, unenthusiastic or unmotivated if passion were their primary value.

Now, for the sake of argument, and argument only... let us say it was you who fell into any of those categories—What now? First and most important is the fact that you have read this far. It means you are in search of a change. It means that you somehow do hold an interest in the profession, a desire that maybe you did not even think you had.

My advice is that it is never too late to become passionate. If you did fall into any of those categories, rather than thinking you are in the wrong profession, I would advise you to consider that probably you have not nourished the proper mentality. Maybe, you have unconsciously created within you a *negative* effect that equally affects the way others perceive you.

Yes, it may be reversible, and you can soon learn how. In the meantime...go ahead, be passionate! Besides, it is free! No membership required, and no sales gimmicks (no pun intended). You won't need to wait for UPS to deliver, and no shipping & handling required. You can enjoy its benefits right away. Once passion becomes part of you, I cannot guarantee you will develop into a celebrity, but you can be darn sure you will be a superstar!

Why Is There A Lack of Passion?

Enthusiasm is an infusion of pure energy that automatically reflects in your voice, your words, and your demeanor; improving the way others perceive you. Frankly, it only happens when you love what you do. Being joyful about your role at work, and what it can offer others, could become a magnetic force that is sure to attract more prospects, getting you closer to your goals each time. I wonder why is it that in sales, passion is not one of the most influential qualities.

As previously mentioned, if we let the mind take control, it would most likely follow the lead of pre-conceived notions. One of those misconceptions, and the most difficult to shed, is that sales is an uphill battle that leaves no room for love or enthusiasm.

Very little has been said about the Creative process in sales. In fact, it is mostly a taboo. I know this because in early years, having read a great number of sales books, I would often encounter material that placed more focus on ways to *"Crush the competition!"* *"Stand ahead of the competition!"* or *"Destroy the competition!"* rather than anything else. None of which is inspirational or remotely uplifting.

I also know it because of the kind of response I gave to some of my co-workers after their positive comments and sincere kudos. They at times wondered what was I doing differently, but I was never able to bring myself to say, *"I am achieving success through the Creative Process."* Seriously, no matter how hard I tried, I could not picture myself saying, *"I'm working from the inside,"* or *"I am creating positive results because I am passionate about what I do."* I felt that replying that way would have earned me a trip to the on-site psychologist, or worst yet, a ticket to a "temporary" vacation.

Instead, I shut up, and every time somebody asked, I would hesitate; but in the end, I would simply say, *"It's all hard work and fighting to keep ahead of the competition."* That was more like it, and it seemed a 'normal' response, so I stuck to it.

A creative mind is set on several key practices: serving others; being helpful; and improving the lives of others through products and/or services. The sales professional does not become a martyr, but rather finds a sense of genuine gratification in her/his work…or just an extra reason to smile.

This specific point reminds me of Jim Carrey's movie, *Yes Man*, in which (focusing on the *life at work* part of the movie) he portrayed a bank employee who was noticeably withdrawn, and with an increasingly negative outlook in life. One day, in response to a challenge placed by the guru at an 'inspirational seminar' he grudgingly agreed to change his usual detached behavior of automatically denying bank loans without caring a bit for other people's needs or dreams, and began approving all of them with an overwhelming 'Yes' each time. After a while, he noticed how his improved outlook and new purpose at work started to make him feel much energized, and how the extra surprising sense of gratification began to positive influence the way his personal life greatly improved.

It is often said that the best description of insanity is doing the same thing over and over again expecting different results each time. Passion does not seem to be a common denominator in sales, while competition is. The reason why we resist a change in our approach to sales may still be taboo and a mystery, but in the end, it could just be insanity!

CHAPTER THREE

＊ ✦ ＊

Choose To Start Your Day Right

Welcome everyday with a smile. Look on the new day as another
special gift from your Creator, another golden opportunity to complete
what you were unable to finish yesterday. Be a self-starter. Let your
first hour set the theme of success and positive action that is certain
to echo through your entire day. Today will never happen again.
Don't waste it with a false start or no start at all.
You were not born to fail.
—Og Mandino

Starting your day right and *choosing to start your day right.* Two phrases
that would surely seem to mean the same, but it is precisely the failure
to notice the difference between one statement and the other what could
keep us from getting closer to reaching target goals and objectives…
especially since one of them means we never took the time to set any.

Sure, a kiss from your spouse, and smooth manageable hair from the
early morning hours are great signs that your day is *starting right*; however,

it is only when you let your awareness to play a key role that you can truly say you are making a choice—*The choice to start your day right.*

If today is a gift ("...*and that is why we call it the present*"—According to the turtle from Kung Fu Panda, the movie) then, the morning should be the time to unwrap it.

Looking back at your Christmas mornings, when it was time to open your presents, how many times did you wish [in your mind] that the one you held in your hands was the very thing you had wished and waited for a whole year? Unfortunately, if you never let your parents know what you wanted... it shouldn't have been a surprise that you never got it. It is no different for us in our daily lives. We only get what we ask for, no more...no less. Consciously or unconsciously, we are creating our experiences.

...And all things, whatsoever ye shall ask in prayer, believing, ye shall receive. Matthew 21:22

Ask + Believe = Receive—Tapping into the Creative to achieve our sales goals is possible, and sometimes even simpler than we *think*. In fact, the quote from the book of Matthew sums it up nicely: *ask, believe, and receive*...in that order. Chapter by chapter I will remind you of the best techniques to use to make this principle work for you.

In the meantime, what goes through your mind after you wake up in the morning? What are some of your first thoughts? Are you conscious of what you are thinking? I know that for some people, the effort goes into figuring out the most effective way to stay in bed for another hour or two. However, making the extra effort to incorporate useful new habits into your routine could undoubtedly boost your productivity and improve your overall results.

The same way breakfast is the most important meal of the day, since it helps kick-start your metabolism, the next few techniques, in the chapters ahead, will help you kick-start your day; and just as with breakfast, these steps will prevent you from running around on mere fumes.

We wrongly tend to believe that the day begins at the office, and all we need to get started is a computer and a comfy chair, without realizing for a moment that the right mindset, infused with a defined set of goals before getting to that desk, could greatly increase our chances for a more productive outcome. It would no longer be Russian roulette. Your accomplishments would be the by-product of a proactive approach.

Get Up Early

"It is well to be up before daybreak, for such habits contribute to health, wealth, and wisdom"—Aristotle

There is a reason that the expression, *the early bird catches the worm*, has withstood the test of time. It is seen in the undeniable correlation between rising early and success. I know from experience that this could be a challenge; however, after you start noticing the results and the positive changes this simple act creates, you, too, will learn to consider it a choice well worth the effort.

I was not always keen on rising early in the morning, unless it was absolutely necessary. I was always okay with the consequences I knew I had to face by not making the effort, but my decision was a conscious one to trade it all for that extra hour in bed. It got so bad that I became immune to the loud buzzer of the alarm clock; my husband was amazed by my ability to completely ignore the sound. He was good at waking up early everyday to get his day started, and that, was a quality we did not share.

Now, about those consequences—They included rushing out the door, speeding up through traffic, arriving barely on time, and missing scheduled calls that were set up for the early part of the day, because I was catching up on other tasks. It was all a disaster, but in a way, it was my normal.

As a side note, rushing belongs to the Competitive. Once you find yourself in a rush you have switched from the Creative back into the Competitive field, where acting hastily brings situations and events that may seem harmless on the surface, but their repercussions can be felt throughout your day. Below are some other situations that can be prevented by the simple act of rising up earlier.

Tardiness
"Tardiness often robs us opportunity and the dispatch of our forces"
Niccolo Machiavelli (1469 –1527)
One of the major "No-No's": The salesperson that shows
up late for business meetings or client appointments
gives the impression of a lack of interest, respect, and
professionalism. Bonuses, potential business, raises, and
promotions are all at risk by the habit of showing up late.

Lack of Organization

"A first rate organizer is never in a hurry. He is never late. He always keeps up his sleeve a margin for the unexpected" Arnold Bennett (1867-1931)

Not having a pen handy to pick up orders, missing pages on the handouts, out of date materials, and not being ready to effectively start your presentation. These are all signs of either a lack of organization, or that soon you will need to look for a new job. Beware!

Wrong Personal Presentation

*"Common sense is genius dressed in its working clothes"
Ralph Waldo Emerson (1803-1882)*

When I was little, my mom used to say, *"As they see you, they treat you."* A simple principle that is entirely relevant to a profession in which personal presentation matters. With only one chance to make a first impression, we are each given the same opportunity to show how much professionalism can be expected from us, based on our appearance alone.

Your personal presentation can be the difference between getting the sale, and wishing you did.

CHAPTER FOUR

Meditation

Some people think that meditation takes time away from physical accomplishment. Taken to the extremes, of course, that's true. Most people, however, find that meditation creates more time than it takes.
—Peter McWilliams

It should not be surprising to know that many of us can hardly find any moment of the day that we can simply use to pause and breathe—A serene and quite moment that we could dedicate exclusively to ourselves with the intention of focusing and reflecting on our own purpose, and in our own being. We seem to carry a burdensome of tasks and expectations placed on us by those at work and even by those whom we love in our personal lives. It seems as if we are in a constant battle to meet everybody else's needs first, while it just becomes very natural to leave our own priorities for last.

This chapter is designed to remind you that no matter how difficult it may seem, it is imperative to make time for ourselves. We have to be able to bring our energies back into focus, which is in essence, one of the many benefits of meditation.

Considered by many to be a waste of time, meditation can actually help the person perform in a more efficient way, saving us more time than it takes. Having a more serene and focused mind can help the individual think more clearly, manage time more effectively, and accomplish tasks proficiently.

Properly performed, meditation can also help you understand yourself and your mind, allowing you to easily recognize your own direction. You will be able to identify your emotions…making it all much easier to change from a negative attitude to a positive one, from stressed to relaxed, from angry to happy… and so on.

Be still for a moment. Close your eyes. Relax your body as you breathe in and out. What I have just described are not only actions that you should naturally perform at some point each day, but also, key activities involved in meditating; actions that, as you can see, may seem rather simple, yet I doubt that many of us manage to incorporate in a daily routine.

Some of the most interesting books written by brilliant minds, and wealthy public figures comment on the benefits they find in meditating. Do they know something we don't know? In essence, meditation is not a luxury reserved for the wealthy. It is a tool accessible to all of us, just like smiling, and enjoying the sun. Yet, somehow, many people don't seem to take advantage of this simple, but powerful practice, that has the potential to positively influence other areas in our lives.

Meditation trains us to concentrate on a single action, idea, feeling, or concept. Being able to focus and direct our energy toward a desired goal can be an invaluable tool for us in sales…or for any other profession for that matter. The major benefit of meditation, however, can be found in the way this simple act can improve our well-being, whether it is used before work, while at work, or after work.

With more than 55,000 doctors and scientists, The Mayo Clinic is the first and largest integrated medical practice in the world, and according to an article found in their website, meditation can wipe away the day's stress and bring with it inner peace. Not only that, the article lists some of the *emotional* benefits of meditation. Some of them include, gaining a new perspective, reducing negative emotions and increased self-awareness (http://www.mayoclinic.com/health/meditation). In other words, meditation is a great tool to reduce the levels of stress and anxiety that can be at fault for the lack of concentration, drive, passion, awareness and other factors that could keep us away from effectively accomplishing our targets and goals.

I have placed this activity right after the topic of *starting your day right*, because I believe that this is a key practice to incorporate from the earliest hours—before we get involved in our day.

I personally avoided meditation believing that it was an extremely difficult task, one that required so much concentration that I would expect to find myself levitating in the middle of the room (that's what happens when you watch one too many movies). What I found out, though, is that meditating is the most relaxing of all activities. It does not require a special setting, or a special position. A comfortable place… somewhere quiet and private will do.

Practice makes the teacher. As you get comfortable with meditation, you will be able to master different and more advanced techniques that you can adjust to fit your own individual purposes, including setting the basis to support your personal development objectives.

Before you start, make sure you choose a comfortable chair, or sit on your bed with your legs crossed and your back against the wall. It is important that you keep your back straight, as this will help with your breathing—an essential part of meditating.

As you improve this skill, you will be able to find your own style and even reach a higher level of performance. For now, though, let's get started at the beginners' level:

- **Just close your eyes and focus on something peaceful and pleasant. Breathe deeply and slowly from your abdomen rather than your chest. You should feel your stomach rise and fall while your chest stays relatively still.**

- **Relax every muscle in your body. It is important not to rush, as it will take time to fully relax. Mentally give permission to your body to release tension, starting at your toes and working all the way up to your head, until all the tension melts away.**

- **Your mind will try to wander. This is natural. Try to at all times keep your attention within you, since it will always try to bounce from thought to thought...the idea is to allow all the "chattering" in your mind to gradually fade away.**

- **Let your attention focus on your breathing. Listen to it. Breathe in three or four heartbeats. Breathe out three or four heartbeats. Again, concentrate on nothing but your breathing. Feel the air flowing into your lungs. Feel the blood flowing through your body. Repeat this procedure until you feel satisfied with your session. Take a last deep breath and open your eyes.**

There you go! It wasn't difficult at all, right? Set aside time, then start meditating. Some people may need just a few minutes to pump up their energies, while others may be able to spend as much time as they like. Take as long as you personally need. There are no time requirements to meet. Make sure that before you get started you turn off all your alarm clocks, take off your watch, and get away from the TV, cell phones, or any other devices that may avert your attention.

CHAPTER FIVE

+—⧓⧗⧓—+

Think Like A Superstar

A man paints with his brains and not with his hands.
—Michelangelo Buonarroti

The concept is very simple. Let us repeat it once more. **We cannot expect positive results with a negative mentality.** We do not necessarily intend to have a negative mentality. It is not something we seek, but it is mostly from conditioning; and if we do not actively try to change, it will continue playing in your mind like a broken record.

High achievers know the importance of changing the internal messages, and keeping negative thoughts off their minds. I would bet that Tiger Woods does not get up in the morning saying, *I hate golf,* and Oprah is not back in her office saying, *I can't stand that screaming crowd today.* The success of these two very influential public figures is not a product of coincidence. They are constantly and proactively setting goals and reaching them through a positive approach.

The same way your body needs training to keep in shape, your mind does, too. That is where affirmations play a key role. Some people reckon them a waste of time, and I cannot blame anybody who does. I was certainly one of them. I never understood how repeating something several times to myself, could make any real difference. I was never a big fan of getting up in the morning and repeating ten times in front of the mirror: "I'm thin, I'm beautiful, and I can sing like Mariah Carey." It not only sounded ridiculous, but impossible. In cases like that, the mind tends to interpret the statements as lies; so the results are sure to be more negative than positive—at least they were for me—I gained weight, and my husband left the room every time I threatened to sing a note.

I later found out that it is not all about words alone but rather the vibrations they produce. The objective is not to tell yourself a lie, but to get excited about the possibilities while they are on their way to becoming your realities.

So how do we know if we are effectively using affirmations to our favor? The answer lies in your emotions. The right statements create feelings of excitement, possibility, and hope.

Let us try an example. Say the following statement to yourself:

—I am the best sales person in the world!

Now, stop for a moment. How did you feel about the statement? Did you feel it to be somehow possible? Most likely, those words did not mean much to you, since it does not sound realistic to start with.

Now, let us try it a different way. Remain aware of any sensations as you say it.

*—I am in the process of becoming the highest and
best-paid producer in the company.*

Now, how did you feel about that statement? Did it create within you the sensation that it was a possibility, and that you could truly be on your way to achieving it? Most likely, you did.

Let us try one more example:
(1) I am a millionaire (2) I have a millionaire mind.

The first statement would most likely work better for you, if you are a millionaire, and it is your goal is to obtain more wealth. If you are not, however, the second statement is for you. Nobody can tell you that you do not have a millionaire mind. Actually, just by stating the second sentence, you automatically place yourself within the realm of having a millionaire mind…and there is no telling what great things you can accomplish with it!

The bottom line is that by making a conscious effort to change negative thoughts, you give your subconscious mind more power to go to work. For that purpose, I have put together a list of affirmations designed for us in the sales profession.

"Human beings, by changing the inner attitudes of their minds, can change the outer aspects of their lives" William James (1842-1910)

My sales skills get better and better every day.

All the money I want comes easily to me doing what I love to do.

I am now creating total financial success.

I am reaching all my goals in a very relaxed way.

I am excited about the possibility of producing
thousands of dollars today doing what I love to do.

My paycheck increases month by month.

I am open to producing massive profits today.

I bless all my customers and those doing business with me.

I am focusing on opportunities rather than obstacles,
and I see my sales grow.

I create the exact level of my financial success.

I am committed to constantly learning and growing.

I can be or do whatever I propose. I am becoming each day,
the most successful person in my field.

I accept all calls from my clients today,
and I look forward to the great things we are doing together.

My work allows me to be successful and wealthy.

My sales potential is not limited.
There is no ceiling on the amount of profit I can create today.

Before every call, I let go of tension and stress,
and I receive the call in serenity.

A "NO" is the start, not the end.
After hearing a "NO", Let the game begin!

I have favor with my boss and coworkers,
and my day is full of positive relations.

Today, I present my passion as a gift to the world,
and I am open to the great wealth of leads and prospects that flow.

My wealth grows in relation to my commitment to helping others.

I am ready and open to receive new business
and exciting opportunities.

I am thankful for the people that are ready
to do business with me today.

I am able to live the lifestyle I desire, thanks to my work.

I bless the company I work for and all my peers and co-workers.

I admire those that are now achieving their goals, and firmly believe
I, too, can meet all my sales expectations.

In review, if you want to increase your financial level, make your consciousness match that same level of prosperity. This is entirely possible by focusing your attention on powerful, positive affirmations, fueled with desire and intention, which is precisely what, makes them effective. The energy they produce is creative. That energy has the capacity to move your mind in the desired direction, producing positive vibrations; and releasing stress that easily builds up throughout a workday.

The affirmations offered above are mostly short and simple statements. Majority of them are only one sentence, and not complicated at all. They can be used at any moment of your day, or whenever you are willing to set aside a minute, or two for your own personal development. Choose the ones that fit best. Better yet, build your own. In fact, I have left some room below for that. Use them to change any broken record you may be working with, and become the superstar you are meant to be.

_____

_____

_____

_____

_____

_____

_____

_____

_____

_____

CHAPTER SIX

━┄ ⊰✧⊱ ┄━

God & Prayer

In the beginning, God created the heavens and the earth.
—Genesis 1:1

We cannot expect to follow the Creative Process without acknowledging the Creator Himself. From the first few words of the Bible, we learn how God *created* the earth. If we keep reading, we learn how what was *dark* became *light*, what was *infertile* became *fruitful*. He saw the need for *expansion*. He created the *heavens* and the *earth*, *morning* and *night*.

Look at some of the highlighted words from the text, and notice how relevant the so-called opposites are, even from the first few words of the Bible. Sometimes you cannot even relate to one without the other. But the real reason why I highlighted those words from the book of Genesis was to emphasize one of the most applicable points I try to make within the pages of this book. Notice how all that was dark or in some way negative, became light and undoubtedly positive after the *influence* of the *Creator*, and as a *result* of *creation*—

two words from which the term *creative* ... as in *Creative* process, derives.

I do understand that for many individuals, the belief in the existence of a Creator is still a challenge. Blame it on the modus operandi of the mind. The common notion, *seeing is believing*, makes faith one of the most extraordinary traits of human beings; and one of the reasons why the Creative process is bound to be considered a challenge as well. So before further introducing the principles that made the Creative process real to me, I wanted to explore the relevance of the Book that carries the primary standards of the process, and its overall application in our modern-day lives. (See appendix A).

After my frustrating experience with many conventional books, it was not only refreshing, but also incredible that it was precisely in the Bible, the book that refers to the creation and the Creator Himself, that I was able to find a majority of the answers I was seeking.

A now famous quote from former president, Ronald Reagan, reads, *"Indeed, it is an indisputable fact that all the complex and horrendous questions confronting us at home and worldwide have their answer in that SINGLE BOOK."* (*Newsweek magazine*—Dec 27, 1982 pg. 46). On a different occasion, he was also heard saying, *"Within the covers of the Bible are the answers for all the problems men face."* It seems as if he strongly believed that the Bible was a very good source for finding answers; and suddenly I get the feeling that I may not be the only person turning to it for answers as well.

Prayer fits in the Creative Process. For professional or personal purposes, it should be considered as one of the greatest ways to connect to that Creative force of the universe. Unfortunately, prayer may have rather become an activity to which we resort mostly in times of trouble and need.

This chapter is strategically placed following the order of acts that I recommend to incorporate. I have intentionally laid out for you the activities that you can advantageously perform from the early hours of your day. You can decide on what sequence they are best for you.... but, how can prayer be applied, if there is no faith? And how can we incorporate the advice from the Bible, if there is no assurance on the basic principle that this book is relevant or even...real?

We can all benefit from prayer, and for that reason, I did not want this chapter to be only for those who have a set foundation of belief, but also for all others who don't. I will make a humble attempt to bring out facts, data, or personal observations that may assist to establish some type of conviction...even if it is only based on simple rationale.

Faith Shaken

Based on data and research some scholars have long agreed that some of the writings in the Bible could date as far back as 3500 years ago. Now to make it even more interesting, it seems that the origins of the Bible may date from much earlier times than previously thought. New discoveries and recent research provides more validity to its claims of being a Book, inspired with information that was ahead of its time.

In January 2010, the discovery of an ancient artifact made national news, including two of the major media outlets, Fox News, and MSNBC. The articles can be found on their respective websites (FoxNews. com—Published January 19, 2010—*When was the Bible really written?* / MSNBC.COM—Published January 15, 2010—*Artifact suggests Bible written Centuries earlier*). The reports suggest that the recent finding defies early assessments, and now researchers hold proof that validates the authenticity and legitimacy of the Bible being an ancient document.

Most likely, we will never know with exactitude how far back this book dates. All we can do is wonder, how a book that was written so long ago, can address so many facts that were only recently confirmed by modern science.

Just to give an example, I chose to consider the information found in the Bible related to *the earth*, keeping in line off course with the topic of creation, and, because without the help of modern inventions, and advanced scientific studies, the Bible clearly and inexplicably stated its shape:

*"It is He that sitteth upon the **circle** of the earth....*
(Isaiah 40:22). KJV

*"He stretcheth out the north over the empty place, and **hangeth the earth upon nothing.** (Job 26:7)—KJV*

No doubt, ages ago, the earth's shape was fully debated among sailors, mathematicians, astronomers, philosophers, inventors, theologians, and just about all great thinkers. In times when views about it ranged from the theory that it was flat, to the notion that elephants and giant turtles held it aloft, the Bible goes as far as to state not only its shape, but also the fact that it was hanging "upon nothing." Those two verses could have solved much sooner, two of the greatest findings established millennia later - Not only its shape, but its gravity.

But the shocking ability of the Bible to foretell and to be ahead of science does not stop there. Some of its verses provide information related to astronomy, geography, oceanography and more. For example, it talks about the stars and constellations, sometimes even by name.[1] It implies the rotation of the earth,[2] and the motion of

---

1   Isaiah 40:26; Psalms 147:4; Job 9:9; Job 38:31-32.
2   Job 38:12-14.

the sun.[3] It clearly refers to the expansion of the universe,[4] which is a relatively recent theory. It reveals the existence of 'paths,' valleys, mountains, and springs below the oceans[5], and it describes the hydrologic cycle[6] as well as other facts of science not discovered, or at least, not confirmed until the development of modern inventions. It all sounds like insider's information… straight from the *'source.'*

Again, maybe it is based on our usual 'seeing is believing' mentality, or it might be thanks to our constant 'quest to know,' but many can approach the Bible with the purpose of finding methodical or at least more logical data; and frustration can easily set after failing to find more tangible facts or explanations. Some simply could lose interest in reading further, while others could completely discard its real application and wisdom. All it takes is a few chapters to realize that the Bible wasn't written to be a scientific thesis or a research paper. More than geography, astronomy, or any other science known to man, what we can find by carefully reading, is that the Bible is about God and His purpose for humankind.

Besides, imperfect hands wrote the information… and some very humble ones, I might add. Looking at some of the characters in the Bible and their professions, we learn that a number of them were very wealthy and politically important men, while others, were shepherds and fishermen who had no possible knowledge of science, and maybe even terrified of what they were being shown.

The message was given to them through visions and inspiration—this according to the comments of the writers themselves. They used the word "visions" or "signs" before introducing some of their points. Based on that explanation, the writer of one of the verses (see above—

---

3   Psalms 19:5-6* Scientists confirm that the sun does in fact moves through space (Aprox.600000 mph).
4   Psalm 104:2; Isaiah 40:22
5   Psalm 8:8; Jonah 2:6; Job 38:16
6   Job 36:27-29; Amos 5:8; Ecclesiastes 1:7

regarding the earth's shape) might have seen in a vision some kind of round-shaped item, and he could have used the word *circle* to describe it. Trying to find argument to the veracity of that description, however, some accuse the Bible of being wrong on several arguments. A rather popular accusation states that a 'plate' or a 'pancake' are both circle-shaped, but flat, and since no further 'scientific explanation' is provided on the subject to confirm that the Bible is actually referring to a sphere-shaped object instead, then, the Bible must be wrong… or at least should not be considered to have its "facts" straight.

God was capable of correcting the writer. Furthermore, to ensure precise scientific accuracy, He could have eliminated the middleman; and instead of giving inspiration and showing visions, He could have written it all Himself. He could have then clearly described the earth's depth, size, circumference, radius, and, dimensions… but should it really take all of this to make us believe?

Maybe God wanted to match the information to our imperfect state, and He, after all, wanted to leave out some of the facts for a higher purpose. Maybe by doing so, He could look at hearts and identify true followers – those who believe, not based on physical convictions, but rather from faith. In the end, all that could be more important to Him than instructing the reader about facts or science. It is His book after all…and the best selling one in history, I might add.

Every way of a man is upright in his own eyes, but God Himself is making an estimate of hearts – Proverbs 21:2.

That verse not only makes it clear that He is truly looking at hearts, but also, explains that God already knew these things would take place…humanity looking at things with their own eyes and becoming "upright" based on their logic -—making them somehow *right* and God…*wrong.*

Based on accounts recorded in the Bible, those who truly believed in Jesus rarely asked for proof. They followed Him by faith. By contrast, the Pharisees and the unbelievers were always asking for miracles on the spot, and demanding of him to provide signs, or some type of tangible proof; with the excuse that only then could they believe He was the Messiah.

They wanted something physical, tangible…facts. It seemed that raising the dead and healing the sick were not enough, they always wanted more. They always expected proof. There are several examples that illustrate those types of encounters between Jesus and his opposers, but no doubt, the most noteworthy accounts occurred at the hour of His execution. In those moments, His opposers and even Herod, himself, asked for a sign (Luke 23:8-9). At the cross, He was nearly accused of being a fraud, as people demanded that He save Himself as proof that He was the 'King of the Jews' (Luke 23:35-38).

…However, the most famous case came while He was on the cross. The account involves two men. On one side, the first man challenged the veracity of Jesus claims of being The Christ, and suggested that Jesus save himself, while on the other side, the other man, also in his darkest hour, and in the same precarious situation as the first, made the decision to believe. He did not make any excuses for himself. Needless to say… to only one of them was paradise promised.

So this is the bottom line: Faith does not translate into science. Once faith is replaced by a concrete reality, it stops being faith and instead, it becomes just another fact.

Thanks to direct communication, Moses was able to ask questions. One of them was about the meaning of God's name, to which The Lord responded: *"I shall prove to be, what I shall prove to be" (Exodus 3:14)*. Rotherham's translation states: *"I will become whatsoever I please"*, and according to King James Version *"I Am that I Am"*. These responses are all verbs that involve the act of *becoming* or *being*. In other words, God tells us that He becomes whatsoever is needed to fulfill His purpose.

Suppose you could become anything, you wanted to become for a purpose… What would you do for your family and friends? Is it possible you could become a cure in case someone became ill…A wealthy benefactor in the event someone else was in need of financial aid? Would you become a person in the right place, at the right time to provide rescue in a moment of danger? Doesn't this already sound to you like the answer to many *prayers*?

If we use prayer in such critical moments of our lives—sometimes even as an automatic, split-second response – why, then, don't we believe that it could have a practical application in the professional and business areas as well?

Ask, and it shall be given you; seek, and ye shall find;
knock, and it shall be opened unto you. (Matthew 7:7)

Use prayer as a way to ask for direction, tranquility, understanding and all the qualities needed to help you succeed in a more relaxed manner. Use it to express your gratitude and appreciation for what you have already accomplished or achieved; and to ask for whatever will help you improve as a person and as a professional. Remember: *"Ask, and you shall receive,"* and prayer is your best channel to accomplish that.

"Work, work from morning until late at night. In fact, I
have so much to do that I shall have to spend the first three
hours in prayer."—Dr. Martin Luther King, Jr.

As I once heard Oprah say on one of her shows, *"God can dream bigger dreams for you that you can dream for yourself."* I recommend prayer to you as a positive addition to your routine, one that could potentially bring you more peace, fulfillment, and intention.

Bible and Wealth

According to a widespread conception, God demands martyrdom, and requires us to rid ourselves of material possessions to become fit followers. In other words, success and wealth are often considered 'unapproved,' and at times even ungodly. It is not a prevalent notion to link wealth and prosperity with God's requirements; and in occasions, it is more common we find people that actually shy away from accomplishments as a way to avoid drifting away from what they believe are God's standards or expectations.

The notion seems to spring from the account found in the book of Luke:

"And a certain ruler asked him, saying, Good Master, what shall I do to inherit eternal life? And Jesus said unto him, Why callest thou me good? None is good, save one, that is God. Thou knowest the commandments, Do not commit adultery, Do not kill, Do not steal, Do not bear false witness, Honor thy father and thy mother. And he said, All these have I kept from my youth up. Now when Jesus heard these things, he said unto him, yet you lack one thing: sell all you have, and distribute unto the poor, and thou shall have treasure in heaven: and come follow me. And when he heard this. He was very sorrowful: for he was very rich. And when Jesus saw that he was very sorrowful, he said, How hardly shall they that have riches enter into the kingdom of God! For it is easier, for a camel to go through a needle's eye, than for a rich man to enter the Kingdom of God"—(Luke 18:18-25) KJV.

I would ask you now, what do you think is more impossible to do: Walk on water, resurrect the dead, ascend to heaven, convert water into wine, heal the sick with just a touch, multiply the bread and feed thousands with provisions for only a few, or make a camel pass through a needle's eye? The answer is all of the above! All of those feats belong to the realm of the impossible, yet Jesus accomplished all of them, with the exception of the last one. Nevertheless, do you really have any doubt that he would have been able to, if he had wanted?

There are cases in Matthew and Luke, in which Jesus teaches that with faith, it is possible to perform miracles that exceed our imagination. He used the examples that included moving trees and even mountains:

"...Verily, I say unto you, If you had faith the size of a mustard seed, you shall say unto this Sycamine tree, Be plucked up by the root, and be planted in the sea; and it should obey you." (Luke 17:6) KJV

Now, that sounds more difficult than opening the hole of a needle! But what is important to note from that scripture is the use of the word *verily* to reinforce His assertion that even though He wasn't performing the miracle right there and there, it was undoubtedly possible.

If we read the account of the rich man a bit further, we find that those who heard Jesus that day asked, *"Who then can be saved?"* He had a simple answer: *"All things impossible to men are possible with God."* That reinforces my original point. It sounds impossible to us for a camel to go through the needle's eye, but *not* to God; therefore, we know that the statement was not a condemnation, rather a caution.

Besides, Jesus never even used the word *impossible*, but rather implied it to be *difficult* or *hard* ...for a rich man to enter the Kingdom of God. Then again, what do you expect? The guy did refuse a formal invitation from Jesus Himself, and rather chose material possessions... you got to admit, he had that one coming.

...And that is precisely where the caution begins. In a previous account from the same book of Luke, Jesus warns, *"No servant can serve two masters; for either he will hate the one and love the other....You cannot be slaves to God and to riches."*

We all know now, which master the rich man chose. Material possessions were not the problem. The love for them was (Timothy 6:10).

The message is quite clear. In modern-times lingo, Jesus could have all narrowed it down to a simple, *'Get your priorities straight!'* He might be trying to tell us that once we make the right decisions, great things could follow..., and that may include wealth. Why should I even conclude that?

Navigating the rest of the Bible, we are reminded of how from the beginning of time, the Creator is all for abundance and prosperity, rather than lack and sacrifice. There is a common theme throughout... He desires to provide us with all the riches and wealth He produced just for us. After all, from the account of *creation* in Genesis we learn how He provided the first man with full dominion and free reign over the world. He filled the earth and then made man sovereign. I would say there is no greater wealth than that!

*"And God said, Let us make man in our image, after our likeness: and let **them have dominion** over the fish of the sea, and over the fowl of the air, and over the cattle, **and over all the earth**, and over every creeping thing that creepeth upon the earth. 27 So God created man in his own image...." (Genesis 1:26)*

We should know that the earth, from the moment of creation was filled with more than fowl and cattle. It was also filled with sapphires, diamonds, emeralds and all precious stones known to man. It seems God thought of wealth even before we knew what it was.

"You were in Eden, the garden of God. Your clothing was adorned with every precious stone—red carnelian, pale-green peridot, white moonstone, blue-green beryl, onyx, green jasper, blue lapis lazuli, turquoise, and emerald—all beautifully crafted for you and set in the finest gold. They were given to you on the day you were created."
Ezekiel 28:13

We see later how His Anointed Ones, the chosen ones, or simply the ones He called friends, enjoyed great wealth, some of them becoming a "Father of Nations," princes, and even kings. I am referring off course to Abraham, Jacob, David, Joseph, and one of the best examples of all, Solomon. In 1 Kings 10:23, we learn that King Solomon was greater in wisdom and riches than any other king of the earth.

Moving ahead, have you seen the accounts of what is described in the Bible as *The Temple of God*? It was to be built and adorned under His command. Let me tell you, the best and most stylish interior decorators and professionals in New York put together, might be hard-pressed to design anything more opulent; and in even greater distress trying to meet God's requirements and specifications, and to match His exquisite taste. Below is a compilation found in the books of 1st Kings and 2nd Chronicles.

And Solomon overlaid the inside of the house with pure gold, and he drew chains of gold across, in front of the inner sanctuary, and overlaid it with gold. And he overlaid the whole house with gold, until all the house was finished. Also the whole altar that belonged to the inner sanctuary he overlaid with gold. In the inner sanctuary he made two cherubim of olive wood, each ten cubits high. Five cubits was the length of one wing of the cherub, and five cubits the length of the other wing of the cherub; it was ten cubits from the tip of one wing to the tip of the other. The other cherub also measured ten cubits; both cherubim had the same measure and the same form. The height of one cherub was ten cubits and so was that of the other cherub. He put the cherubim in the innermost part of the house; and the wings of the cherubim were spread out so that a wing of one touched the one wall, and a wing of the other cherub touched the other wall; their other wings touched each other in the middle of the house. And he overlaid the cherubim with gold.

He carved all the walls of the house roundabout with carved figures of cherubim and palm trees and open flowers, in the inner and outer rooms. The floor of the house he overlaid with gold in the inner and outer rooms. For the entrance to the inner sanctuary he made doors of olive wood; the lintel and the doorposts formed a pentagon. He covered the two doors of olive wood with carvings of cherubim, palm trees, and open flowers; he overlaid them with gold, and spread gold upon the cherubim and upon the palm trees. So also he made for the entrance to the nave doorposts of olive wood, in the form of a square, and two doors of cypress wood; the two leaves of the one door were folding, and the two leaves of the other door were folding. On them he carved cherubim and palm trees and open flowers; and he overlaid them with gold evenly applied upon the carved work. He built the inner court with three courses of hewn stone and one course of cedar beams. In the fourth year the foundation of the house of the LORD was laid, in the month of Ziv. And in the eleventh year, in the month of Bul, which is the eighth month, the house was finished in all its parts, and according to all its specifications. He was seven years in building it.

Even looking back to some of the gloomiest days, wealth has been part of God's arrangement. He prepared a land for His people. His plan was to lead them out of *slavery*, into *freedom*; and before Moses had any chance to accept the challenge, God commanded that the kids were to be provided with gold and silver. (Exodus 3:22). The articles were to be put on the them. Children were to become the new generation to inherit the land, the first issue at hand was to raise their worth and improve their mentality. They were to be landowners, and masters; there was no room for a slave mentality from that point forward. He did promise them a land of *abundance* after all. It was their *lack* of faith that left them wandering in the desert for forty years.

The examples provided above are only a few; however, in those accounts, we find proof of provision, wealth, and abundance; and those instances make it clear that the Creator wants us to *prosper*, and not to *lack*.

Remember the equation—Ask + Believe = Receive. That verse in Matthew encourages to *"ask"* in prayer. Prayer could be after all, the primary way for us to connect to that source of abundance, and we are welcome to it, based on the words of two of His best friends, King David (Psalms) and King Solomon (Proverbs)

"Commit thy way unto the Lord, trust also in Him;
and He shall bring it to pass (Psalms 37:5)

"Commit thy works unto the Lord, and thy thoughts
shall be established". (Proverbs 16:3)

I think it is time we stop ignoring the real possibility that there could be a greater connection between God and success. I think the notion that The Creator disapproves of financial increase, and that reprimand is in place for it, is one belief worthwhile re-examining. We may actually find out that it could be the complete opposite.

"The blessing of the Lord, it maketh rich, and he addeth
no sorrow with it" (Proverbs 10:22) KJV

CHAPTER SEVEN

—•—◄◊►—•—

Think Big, Dream Bigger, Visualize!

Some people dream of success while others wake up and work harder at it.
—Unknown

Close your eyes. Engage in a little bit of concentration—and now, think of a lemon. Most likely, you will feel your mouth water. Now, think of your favorite meal... the flavor, the aroma, the texture. Did I just manage to make you hungry? If I did, then you just visualized.

Visualization is more than merely thinking. It is the creation of mental images. These images can become something similar to a visual perception – one that can involve feelings; and according to some reports, even the engagement of some of your five senses. What is incredible is that most often, visualizing does not require much effort.

We have seen the many interviews with famous personalities. The show host asks his guest stars what seems to be now a very common question: *"Did you ever imagine you could be this successful?"*

On an overwhelming number of occasions the answer is, *yes*. The rest of their reply may vary, but somehow they manage to be very similar: *"I remember when I was little; I would pick up a comb and sing." "I imagined myself performing in Times Square; I could almost hear the screaming crowd…" "I would stand in front of the mirror and model…" "I had this vivid image of my name on the big screen…"* It is more than a coincidence that the answers are often very similar. They tapped into the same power; and it seems as if all they had to do was daydream.

You might have heard the principle: *Energy flows where attention goes.* The question is, how can we expect to reach our desired goals and aspirations, if we don't place enough attention on them? That is the job of visualization.

I could tell you how visualization has positively improved my results, but remember it is all about you, your profession, and even your personal place in life. What makes you smile? What are your dreams and aspirations? Where do you want to go, and how far? Consider it your map.

I choose to visualize as I am setting my personal goals for the day. I can do this in different ways, or at different times of the day. Personally, I like setting my goals based on desired number of transactions, or on specific profit amounts—so I usually start by saying, *today my goal is $_____*. Then to reach that certain objective, I tend to visualize factors and situations that could assist me in making it happen, or that could help me bring to mind the way I feel after certain achievements. If your field demands that you set your personal goals the same way, then your questions should be *what* or *how much* you would like to produce. Try to keep it realistic. Remember the idea is that you could sense them as an actual possibility. After all, I did say, "daydream"…not "hallucinate."

There are different techniques you could apply to use visualization in your favor. The following is one example of the many ways I do it, based on my work in cruise vacation sales:

At any moment of the day, I might take a minute and use it to envision the many thousands of couples and families who board one cruise ship or another every week. Some of the newer ships can accommodate over five thousand people. There are over five major cruise lines in the US alone, and each line has a minimum of five to ten vessels…and on most occasions, they are sold to capacity.

Based on that scenario, I bring to mind the steady and guaranteed flow of sales that is commonly generated. On occasions, I imagine that ten of those couples boarding ships bought their cruise line tickets from me. Does it sound crazy? Not until you try it.

We are talking about using visualization to our advantage and choosing abundance thinking. What are ten couples when there are thousands of potential customers available? Those ten couples booking with me daily, however, do automatically increase my bottom line, and place me on a good spot on the board. The most important thing, it reminds me that there is truly no lack, and no reason to miss my goals for that day. I personally choose to see abundance, and endless possibilities.

Once, having a conversation with Jackson, a sales agent I briefly met in a training class, I commented about my personal experience with this exercise. He sounded interested and said he wanted to hear more. I went on to explain how amazing my day turns out when I find a certain situation or source where I envision abundance. I told him that it proves to be a great help every time I do. He said he wanted to try it. He added he didn't know what his "source of abundance" would be, but that he would certainly try to find it. We exchanged phone numbers, since I told him I wanted to follow up and see how he was doing.

Weeks later, he sounded like a much different person on the phone. With excitement in his voice, he started to explain how astonished and encouraged he was. He mentioned how this simple exercise, with not much effort, has absolutely increased his production, and improved his overall results. I wanted to hear more!

I asked him, what his source was. He went on to explain how once flying from Fort Lauderdale back to Arizona from visiting his parents, he saw through his airplane window, like the rest of us while flying over a major city, a vast array of tiny sparkles of light running for what appeared to be endless miles. He thought to himself how each sparkle meant a house, a building, a vehicle, all full of people amounting to the thousands.

If he was consciously looking for the so-called source of abundance… he found it. He was reminded that there was never a lack. When he thinks back to those lights, and envisions only twenty out of the thousands of people on the ground, calling in any given day at the office, he can sense days filled with unlimited sales opportunities.

He laughed about how on his way to work, he now looks forward to his "twenty sparkles"—While, he realizes that this is not always the case, he said, he can appreciate how much more "peace" he feels going into the office; and how the noticeable increase in his sales transactions "doesn't hurt," even though he couldn't understand why.

I was not ready to explain to him back then, but I am certainly ready now.

He was experiencing the results of working under the Creative. By remaining positive and excited about the possibilities, he automatically created within himself feelings of expectancy, assumption, and enthusiasm. The positive thoughts he embraced and believed in, became positive experiences. He felt the sensation that he no longer had to struggle with the usual negative thoughts of lack; in return, lack was not part of his day at work. (Uff! I hope he reads this book. I lost his number).

Moving on…Visualizing and setting my goals for the day has also helped me tremendously, because it puts into perspective the feeling of fulfillment I get from any single sale, and reminds me to reach higher. It is my personal goal; I am not competing with anybody else's. Neither are you.

Now, to elaborate…It is common to get a gratifying sense of fulfillment after one single sale, so it is possible we could kick back and think that the one sale was enough to make our day. In other words, we could get so comfortable that even though potential transactions are smacking us on the side of the head, we are not placing any real effort on closing them. That happens mostly when we fail to set goals. That is the reason why incorporating this step is so essential.

I remind you that anybody can set goals, but setting them in a way that encompasses vision or simply infusing them with emotions is what is bound to place you in a creative mode. That addition to you routine should be considered one of the best ways to set the day in motion, but the reality is that visualizing can be helpful at any hour of the day. In fact, it is not an activity entirely exclusive to setting the usual daily goals, but it can be used to achieve even greater objectives in business and in life—As great as a business empire, for example.

Yes, some individuals utilize the concept as a way to *think big!* It would seem as if for those who achieve extraordinary success, thinking big comes naturally. *Donald Trump* should be one of the most fitting examples. For many of us, elevating our mentality is a skill that improves with practice. For others, *thinking big* may be an act that could take them out of their own comfort zones, since it is far off from their typical everyday thinking patterns; but a case like that of *Trump* and others like him reminds us that keeping higher goals and dreams in mind should be as easy and as natural as breathing. For them, it is something that you might as well just do.

> *"I like thinking big. If you're going to be thinking,*
> *you might as well think big."*
> —Donald Trump

Where do you want to go? What do you want to accomplish? Whatever the answer, the purpose is to sense and visualize yourself in the desired situation…not yet a reality…but a true possibility. In the end, the answer to some of those questions may surprise you. One day you may want to have a promotion, escape to Fiji, or who knows? Maybe just as I did, your answer may be, "I want to write a book!" (By the way, if you are reading this book, and you are not my mom, what you are holding is proof that the process works).

CHAPTER EIGHT

━┥ ⅀◈⅀ ┝━

The Power Of Words And Good Communication

*Properly practiced creativity must result in greater sales
more economically achieved. Properly practiced creativity
can lift your claims out of the swamp of sameness and make
them accepted, believed, persuasive, and urgent"*
—William Bernbach

The words we use matter! The candidates that can better express their values and ideals win; therefore, presidents and leaders are elected. It is with the right or wrong choices of words that arguments are started or avoided, marriages are strengthened or fall apart, wars are averted or get started. It is with words that you can get people to do what you ask, get them to agree with a point of view; and it is only with words that people can ultimately buy what you are selling.

I personally think there should be a class in high school dedicated to the effective use of words. That area could make our kids more prepared to face the real work-related situations that they will be sure to encounter on a near future. Having the proper communication skills, could make it easier for them to build better business relations; perhaps avoid a few shut doors, and even the possibility of evading one or two heartbreaks when it came to their personal lives.

While we hope and dream that the topic will soon be part of our kids curriculum, allow me to briefly remind you the importance of words in the sales field, and the reason why effective communication is so essential to the profession:

- o   To keep the customer engaged in your product and presentation
- o   To get them excited and involved
- o   To trigger a positive response from your customers
- o   To elevate their curiosity to learn more about your products and services
- o   To put the customer at ease with your product

The way we use our words can trigger emotional responses. Words have the *power* to persuade, manipulate and control others; sometimes even without their knowledge.

What we say also has the power to create impressions, images, and expectations. It can help us influence decisions, and build connections as well. Whether you want to win an argument or just sell more, using the right set of words will lead you to accomplish just that. Used poorly, however, they can have an opposite effect, like lowering expectations, kill interest and enthusiasm, and even cause the consumer to hold off.

CONNECTING WHAT YOU SAY WITH THE CREATIVE PROCESS

It is often said that the customer does not care until you care. One of the major ways to show interest for their needs and willingness to help is through words. The proper communication, along with the right attitude and demeanor could create a connection that builds not only a client, but also a relationship.

It is easy to find sales professionals who choose to talk fast, rush the conversation, and ignore the customer's needs, in order to push his or her own point of view. What is going to sound amazing is that in a majority of cases, the salesperson is doing all that without even noticing…having minimal awareness. That is just some of the effects of working within the wrong process.

The daily struggles to keep up with co-workers achievements or the desire to match up to other people's expectations are just some of the situations that drive the individual to get in high gear. In an effort to meet those set standards, the person tends to forget about the most important task at hand: Servicing the customer, which in exchange is the best chance to creating a 'connection' with the customer.

…Connection? Some may call it chemistry; but how important is it? I can only say that if having chemistry is so important for major things in life such as marriages, friendships, business partnerships, and even to tango, how much more important could it be when it comes to a sales transaction? I say this reminding you that in most cases, you, and the client start as complete strangers, and no matter how many sales tactics, strategies, or pitches you are trained to pull from up your sleeve… nothing is going to move forward until a certain connection is established.

89

A connection between you and your customer can automatically set you apart from the competition without much effort. It can be so important and powerful that price may no longer be the decision-making factor. Even after the customers' attempt to shop around for prices, there are greater chances that they would turn around and decide to award their business to the person with whom they felt most comfortable.

Trust is the major element involved in creating a connection, and it is mostly through words and effective communication that you can reassure your customer that it is safe to place confidence not only in your product, but also in you, as a professional.

A way to measure the level of success of that connection is by observing how the conversation flows. You know that you are on the right path when the customer shows that she/he is comfortable enough to share her/his needs, ideas, thoughts and even one or two stories.

Incorporating the right set of words into the process, along with the right attitude and mentality is essential. The wrong set will keep you frustrated and asking why the customer chose to do business with somebody else. You could be left scratching your head and wondering how is it possible that you had better prices, location, and even a more popular company name, logo, as well as a bunch of goodies…and they still opted for the next guy.

CHAPTER NINE

Putting It All Together. From Beginning To End, Steps To Close The Sale

You could have good communication skills, but if you display the wrong attitude, others will simply sense what you say as empty words. You could have a fantastic attitude, but if you find yourself saying the wrong things... it could only land you in hot water! You could be repeating affirmations twenty times a day, but if your attitude and words are not in-sync with your newfound mentality, you are just wasting your time.

This chapter focuses on the steps needed to keep on the right track in relation to your words and attitude, while performing in the actual sales process. Previous and upcoming chapters that focus in your inner qualities should serve as the foundation to properly connect your mindset with what you say (words) and how you decide to act (attitude). Those two latter ones, words and attitude, are at the forefront of your performance. Properly executed, you can use them to create a favorable impression with your client.

GREETING

As the saying goes, *"There's never a second chance to make a first impression."* It is in the greeting that this adage applies best. You will find your greatest chance to *create* a customer out of a prospect precisely at the first point of contact.

Attitude: life is unpredictable. At any given moment, negative or stressful situations may come up and bring a person's mood down, and with that, the possibility that the individual's attitude can shift from welcoming to unwelcoming. But even when we are faced with life's challenges, we still retain our power. We can choose to act happy or stressed, to sound sad or excited. We have the control. We hold the key. The key I remind you, is self-awareness.

Those with the right mentality, or at least, those armed with awareness, will have an increased chance of putting negativity behind, 'shake it off,' and get ready for the initial encounter. Again, it is only with awareness that we, as individuals are capable of identifying our own emotions and applying the necessary changes, especially as we approach a step in the process that could erroneously be considered trivial. Truth is, the *greeting* has the highest potential to assist the individual build rapport, so let's keep these pointers in mind:

o   The simple act of smiling makes the difference. The customer can sense it and appreciate it even if the conversation is occurring on the phone. Opening up the call, or starting a face-to-face meeting with a smile automatically lightens the mood, and improves the flow of interaction.

o   Dismissing the importance of this step is what places you at a high risk factor for sounding robotic. It is no secret that some of us may have a one-or two-phrase greeting that is parroted every time we pick up the phone, or any time a new customer walks through the door. By offering your name and properly welcoming your potential clients, you set the vibe that would help the customers decide right from the start if you are the kind of person that they would feel comfortable dealing with... or not.

o   Approach this step with the mentality that you are at the brink of starting a relationship. It is exactly that sense of purpose that could positively influence the rest of the call.

Words: *"I'm glad you stopped by today," "How can I be of assistance?" "We are pleased you called today," "It's our pleasure to further assist you."* These are all obvious, but what truly makes them effective is an energy-infused attitude, a vibrant tone of voice, and when applicable, eye contact—this is the first signal of confidence.

DISCOVER

Yes, you want them to hand you the Discover, and you take Visa and MasterCard, as well. Before getting to that point though, you must first get the facts straight. A sincere understanding for the customer's needs would undoubtedly smooth the way when it comes to picking up any type of credit card. This step involves a series of open-ended questions that could allow you to dig deeper and uncover what your client truly needs...or wants.

Discovery is one of the steps in the process that could make you shine and maybe even to *set you apart*. This is your opportunity to show the customer that you care, and that you are interested in meeting their needs. Some professionals may attempt to sell the product that they would consider appropriate for their client, based on popularity, profit, or maybe to move a certain inventory, while ignoring their customer's basic necessities, preferences, style, age group or any other relevant factor. As a person under the Creative, you will surely benefit from this type of individual, if they so happen to be your competition.

Show you care by listening and not interrupting. Keep eye contact or, if you are on the phone use subtle expressions that indicate you are present and focused on what they are saying. Discovery could be as hard or as simple as you want it to be. Take the right steps:

o With the customer's best interest at heart, it is your mission in this step to find the right match for your client. Getting the proper information will prevent you from trying to sell an adventure trip to a person with mobile disabilities or a Hummer to an environmentally conscious person.

o Don't always assume that the customer is in the mood to answer or that they would automatically become an open book. It is recommended that before you get started, you ask for their permission to proceed with a few questions. Most of them will not see a problem sharing information with you after that. Some may even appreciate your efforts to further assist.

o Ask open-ended questions. You are not doing yourself any favors by asking the customer questions that require a simple *yes* or *no* for an answer. Open-ended questions will definitely 'squeeze' more information out of your prospect—Information that will ultimately help you.

o Do active listening. Write down what they are saying. There is nothing more annoying for the customer than being asked something that they have already answered and nothing more counterproductive for you since time can be your best ally, but going around in circles isn't the most effective way to use it.

o   Use questions that evoke emotions. Remember, emotions are a great part of the basis for the Creative process. You can infuse emotions into any question. As an example, instead of asking, *what car are you looking for?* You could ask, *what is your dream car?* There is more than a slight difference in these two questions. Even though the car of their dreams may be a far reality at that moment, you have undoubtedly managed to stir within them a desire, a memory, or a feeling that could positively affect the outcome.

Words: The *W's* are your friends…I am referring to the *what, when, which, who, where,* and even *how's* in your questioning. Remember to use them to ask questions able to evoke emotions. You can do this regardless of your product: *"What did you love most about your last vacation?", "Which one is your favorite newspaper section to read while sipping your coffee in the morning?", "When do you plan to get away from it all and enjoy one of our amazing packages? "How do you envision you dream wedding?"*

PRE-QUALIFY

Now that you know what they are truly looking for…Can they afford it? Are they ready to commit? Is this really a potential sale in the making? I know what I have said about *relationships* and *connections.* It all sounds wonderful, but it has never been my intention to show you a Dreamland. Keeping it real, we are still in the business of making a profit and time is gold. Connections take time to build, and they do require effort. This process would essential allow you to focus your time and energy on the right prospects.

Attitude: This is the step that some may consider the hardest, to the point that it is commonly ignored or skipped. What is the right thing to say? I personally don't think it is a great idea to be so direct as to ask, *do you have money to pay for this car?* but In essence it is one of the factors we are undoubtedly trying to find out. That is when the right set of words and attitude will play a key role:

o   Do not judge a book by its cover. This step somehow reminds me of Julia Roberts' character in *Pretty Woman* shopping on Rodeo Drive. (…Do you remember the look on the sales clerk's face, after realizing the potential sale lost? Ouch!) This process will essentially help you avoid dismissing a customer merely on the way they look, talk, or act. Instead of judging based on external factors, pre-qualifying will easily allow you to 'get to the bottom of it' by asking a few basic questions. Remain objective, and at no time disregard a potential customer regardless of the exterior. Remain welcoming and willing to assist.

o   It is not 'cherry picking.' The idea is to effectively qualify your customers. You have learned a few things from them already, but before you can even think about saying, "Next!" this step will provide you with a more efficient evaluation of the sales potential. Direct your questions to finding out information related to the cash amount they are willing to spend, or if the person you are talking to is the actual decision maker.

o   If in person, provide your business card. If on the phone, make sure that you have asked them to write down your name, telephone number, extension, and your working hours. You will soon find out if the encounter results in a sale, but in case it didn't, you have automatically increased your chances for future business. They now know how to reach you, and based on how you have handled yourself so far...*Why would they need to go anywhere else?*

o   One of the main purposes is to find out if what you offer matches up to their needs. The answer determines if you are the right person to assist them, or if they need to be referred to somebody else. As much as you would like to have their business, it makes no sense to waste their time...or yours.

o   Always ask the questions respectfully and appropriately.

Words: It is here that people tend to use words like *budget* for example. This gives me a chance to remind you of the importance of using the right words. Budget implies a limit. It describes a set amount of money for a specific purpose. A better option could be the word, *investment*. It implies less of a *limit* in the spending, since the person perceives that buying the product will produce a greater return (...or benefit). What is your *budget* for this trip? Or, how much are you willing to *invest* in your family's vacation? They both mean the same...but the latter one is more effective.

Again, be respectful in your questioning. Expressions to use in this step include the following: *Would you be open to.... Would you be able to...? Is it possible for you to...? I was wondering if...?* In this step of the process, a simple *yes* or *no* answer will do.

PAINT THE PICTURE

No need to be an artist, and no messy brushes or painting involved. In our profession, we perform this step in the process with words, and effective communication. It is what ultimately sells the product.

Many think of this as the easiest step, especially those who 'know their product.' They can go on and on, non-stop about the brands available, the variety of colors, memory capacity, and more—But now that the customer knows the material, size, date of issue and place of origin…how about if we actually paint the picture?

This step is equivalent to the success attained by the realtor able to guide the prospect in visualizing the kids playing in the backyard, the friends laughing in the kitchen, the comfort of having an extra room in the house to handle their business away from the kids' tantrums. What a delight! This is a place the client could soon call home; and as important as a new office or extra closets are, those features do not enhance the experience as much as a good reminder of the many *joys* of personal space.

Painting the picture is all about the benefits involved with your service or product not the features. It is your key to a better and stronger presentation.

Attitude: Use your imagination. There are tons of features to inform your customer about, and highlighting how they can each potentially benefit your prospect may be a challenge, but worthwhile. Be prepared in advance, as to what they are.

o   Your facial expression is important. Do you imagine telling your customer how much fun the kids can have in that pool, when you look bored yourself? Being robotic defeats the purpose. Be excited for them!

o   Here is your chance to prove you were listening. Thanks to the discovery step, you learned how much they enjoy wine, or how often they leave town to visit their parents. You can now mirror that information back to them in the shape of solutions.

Be sure to highlight the benefits of the product and services in that exact area.

o   Feel free to add value to the benefits by offering any type of promotion pertaining to the product or service.

o   Keep a level of enthusiasm in your voice.

Words: Use words that sell the *power* not the just the engine. Highlight the *luxury of the interior* rather than the leather seats. Help them understand the *savings* associated to the vehicle's fuel efficiency. Emphasize *the convenience of service* that comes with around the clock hours, or home delivery. Use *Pampering* instead, if highlighting features such a spa. Inspire them to envision the *trip of a lifetime*, rather than just another vacation. Other words to use in your presentation are, *freedom, envy, peace, purpose, trust, comfort, and relax*, among others.

TRIAL CLOSE

A trial close is possible after any kind of presentation, but it is most effective after a strong one… and you did just that. So now, you may ask the customer, *"How does that sound to you?"* It is that simple.

This step is designed to determine how far or near they are to a purchasing decision. Consider it a test, or a low-risk strategy to trigger a response that will indicate their level of readiness. If done in an untimely or unsolicited manner, you may actually annoy the customer, since they may not be ready to make a decision; and even when they are, they sometimes do not want to show any signals of interest. Performing the trial close after offering the benefits is not at all intrusive. In fact, in some cases, the prospect does not even realize that they are answering to your request.

As simple as this step may seem, it is vital to make the sale go forward. Be on your best game:

Attitude: Keeping up the same level of enthusiasm makes for a smooth transition from the presentation to the trial close.

o   After asking the question, be silent. Do not interrupt. Here is where you let the customer do the talking. They are about to provide you with valuable information...even if they don't say anything. Watch their gestures and body language. The way the customer answers or behaves will provide you with the buying signals. (See insert below).

o   Regardless of how you perceived their response—as negative or positive – do not show frustration or over-excitement. Remember, you are there for their best interest, not your own. Besides the trial close is not a final *yes* or *no*. It is not the end of the process and you may still get a chance to further discuss your proposal without major risks of ruining the sale.

Words: While I do prefer to ask, *how does it sound to you?* Here are other options I recommend: *Does everything sound good? Are we on the right track? Does this make sense? How are we doing so far? Is this what you had in mind? Is this all going to work out for you?*

BUYING SIGNALS

Any verbal or non-verbal agreement such as nods or noises.

Body language that indicates interest such as: Leaning forward, eyes lightning up, and upward changes in the tone of voice, and facial expressions.

Prospect shows interest in the product presented by asking more questions.
Wants to know about the price.
Client asks another person's opinion.
And the ultimate signal, will be your customer reaching for their wallet

NEGATIVE SIGNALS
Customer does not provide a straight answer
Backs away
Does not make eye contact
Seems uninterested after your presentation
Moves from one product to the other without specific interest
And the worst signal. The now famous *"Not now"* excuse

GIVE THEM THE PRICE

In the customer's mind at this point, there is one more thing they need from you, and that is *price*. Now more than ever, people care about cost. Today, the chances are higher that you could encounter a customer who initially approached you with the sole purpose of finding a "good deal." While teens in this age and era are open to meeting new *BFF's* (Best Friends Forever), your customer in this same time and era could not be opposed to finding their *AFF's* (Affordable, Functional, and Fabulous).

This step is very straightforward. They now have all the options available to them, and all the information needed to make a decision; and as I just mentioned, price, on occasion matters, but it would definitely *not* be the final deciding factor.

I say that because the information in this book is designed to give your customer value that goes beyond price. By means of your attitude, personality, demeanor, and efforts to meet their real needs, you have automatically provided a value that transcends a price tag. This is the point where many other books in the market would recommend that you *"sell value, not price."* But I don't have to…you already have.

People buy from people they like. It is less likely they would hesitate to give their information and credit card number to somebody they trust. You may not get every single sale, and not every encounter will result in a "Yes!" but you have undoubtedly set yourself apart and somehow increased your chances to attract and create more sales. That is the benefit of working under the Creative.

The sales process must flow, and you should always do what feels right based on each individual encounter. After providing the price, two things tend to happen. Either you remain quiet, or you could do a second trial close, by asking something like, *is that ok with you?*

Some say that remaining quiet after stating the price can create an awkward silence. This can be true if the customer shows no interest, or if the prospect feels unable to afford the price. Truth be told, if the customer's level of enthusiasm is on track, and everything else works out, don't be surprised if they themselves ask you to run their credit card and close the deal right on the spot.

But don't feel discouraged if that wasn't your case or if you got any type of negative response. The reality is that *'price'* is one of the most typical excuses—right after the *'I have to talk to my spouse'* one, off course—and at times, it is not because of lack of money but because it is an easy one. Customers nowadays are savvy enough to know that using the price as an excuse is a convenient way to 'brush you off' when they don't feel ready. Legitimate reasons for their rejection may not be in their pockets, but rather, in two other major factors: execution... or competition.

Lack of trust, value, quality, or plain lack of information, would be part of the execution flaw; and your *competitors'* prices, location, or variety of products may give you a run for your money, but none of those two issues should have been your major roadblocks. I do however think that there are instances in which you could benefit from two other major strategies. *Creating urgency* and *future referrals* can not only make a difference, but they can also change the game. An upcoming chapter will provide more information. In the meantime, proceed to the next step.

ASK FOR THE SALE

Why guess when you can properly ask? This step is a formal request to close the deal. It is in this step that they will give you a more straightforward commitment, or a more direct objection. This step is essential. There are people in the profession who are terrified to ask for the sale. They feel comfortable enough to perform every step in the sales process but they freeze when it matters most. This is a major signs that the individual is working under the Competitive; where fear of rejection is a by-product, not an intention…but you already knew that.

We don't get credit for a sale that 'almost' happened and we don't have a sale until we get that credit card. So go ahead…ask!

Attitude: Be open to their response, and do not automatically assume a negative outcome.

o   Relax! If you don't make the conscious decision to lighten up and be open to their answer, it will be easy to let pressure build up. It is then when we see the salesperson's tendency of becoming abrasive. Some can see the *"No"* coming out of the customer before they even open their mouths. Remain positive, and relax!

o   Listen! What follows is a straight answer, followed by one or the other: The exciting reason why they are buying, or a string of excuses. You still need to listen.

o   The fundamental inner ability associated with this step is *confidence.* Believe in your value as a sales professional. You spent time explaining the product and you even made them excited about its benefits. If you don't get that credit card…somebody else will.

Words: The most effective way to ask for the sale is to assume the sale. Your chances are better when you give the costumer a choice, instead of the easy way out of a yes-or-no answer. Example: *Would you prefer I order the green or the blue one for you? Are you using a Visa or a MasterCard? When do you want this delivered? Is your name spelled with a double L?*

The *W's* are as effective. They also provide a choice—*Which Credit Card would you use today? What names do you want to put down for your reservation? Which one would you prefer to buy?*

There is no wrong way to ask for the sale, as long as you ask. Here are other examples—*Are you ready to go ahead and book? How about if we start your reservation now? Would you like me to get the paperwork started? Can I proceed with your purchase?*

FEAR OF OBJECTION

Reacting has no place in the Creative Process, so STOP. It is a standard course of action to face a negatively perceived situation with a negative attitude. Remember, negativity begins in your mind. The aggressive and often abrasive response of the salesperson is no more than a projection of the internal being.

The key to remaining in the Creative field lies in your awareness. Staying optimistic and upbeat in the face of rejection opens up a more positive base of interaction between you and the customer. You find more freedom to face a negative response with traits you would not be able to develop otherwise, such as clarity to find solutions, humor to lighten up the mood, and boldness to help you press forward rather than letting go. Insight, persistence, openness, peace, purpose, logic, They all go out the window.

These are all potential qualities available to you under the right mentality and frame of mind. These qualities become the difference between positive outcomes and a disappointing string of experiences. Everybody likes a winner and a "No" should not turn you into the opposite. Have the mentality that a NO is not the end. It is when the games begin.

FACE THE OBJECTION

I hope that the answer you received from the last step was a resounding *"Yes!"* But in case it wasn't, then, this is the step that follows.

Based on your discovery, and pre-qualification, you have a certain assurance that your product is what they want or need. You also sensed their excitement after your presentation, and based on the trial close, and the fact that the customer is still talking to you this far, you know they are still somewhat interested. ….So, what in the world is holding them? There could be a few reasons, and it is only appropriate to face them.

Attitude: First off, remain polite. If you are in control, you will avoid sending signals with body language or facial expressions that show some type of frustration, or worse yet, saying something that the customer can perceive as rude. The steps presented in this chapter are designed to present you as someone who has the customer's best interest in mind. Showing signs of aggravation or annoyance will only state otherwise. You are in control when you remain calm and maintain flow by showing the same energy you started with.

- o Be empathetic. Show understanding for whatever situation is holding them off; even if it is as simple as the excuse that they left the wallet at home, or as complicated as a mid-day soap opera.

- o Be direct with the questions you ask after you show your understanding for their answer.

- o Maintain eye contact. It is very easy to lose confidence after a rejection, but this is no time to retreat. By maintaining eye contact, you show that you are still interested in their business, and that you are ready to do your best to further assist and to help them with whatever is keeping them from going forward.

o   Use Humor. Sometimes all the customer needs is to feel at ease. Regardless of the situation, humor lightens up the mood.

Words: To show you empathize with your customer's situation, you can use expressions such as: *"I understand…" I'm with you..." "I sometimes feel the same way…" "It makes sense…."*

Once you have shown your understanding, it is proper to ask *"Besides this [reason or issue] is there anything else keeping you from booking/buying/ reserving today?"*

CONQUER THE OBJECTION

The final step will also be your opportunity to bring the customer back in track. Now that you know what is stopping them, you can still help them. This is essentially the last chance you have to close the deal.

Using the scenario based on the purchase of a high-end home theater system, for example, the customer may be very excited about the latest technology and the thought of watching his favorite action movie in the comfort of his own home with the same quality of experience he would get in a movie theater. He is sold! However, he will not move one finger until his wife approves such a "self-indulgent" choice.

As an example, the sales agent could then offer the customer the option to go ahead with the purchase, and worst-case scenario, if his wife does not approve, reassure that it is fully refundable within the next thirty days. (Always keep in mind the return policies that apply to each specific case). Probably at some point in the discovery, the customer commented that his wife enjoys going to the movies as much as he does, so the salesperson can now point out that *"this is a must-have item,"* and that there is no doubt that this is a product she would also enjoy.

Using a different type of scenario involving scheduling or reservations—like resorts, excursions, or any other type of travel, the customer may object that they would love to go, but they are not sure of what dates will match their kid's vacations, and they won't be able to find out until next month. Well, (if applicable) you can always advise them that they book the date that appears to be the most convenient for the moment. Highlight the benefit involved in doing that, like holding the best price, or avoiding the hustle of having to spend more time trying to book it later. Reassure, however, that without further penalties they can make the change, if needed, by making one simple phone call (Watch out for penalty dates).

That type of solution applies to selling other services that involve planning, like wedding and birthday celebrations, or any other kind of event.

It is appropriate to ask for the sale again. Ask for the credit card number one more time. You would be astonished to see how some solutions as simple as they seem, can make a world of difference. Once the prospect realizes that the purchasing procedure is not as difficult, complicated, or as final as it seems, there is a chance that their *"No"* will become the *"Yes!"* that you were going for.

CHAPTER TEN

+ ⚎ +

Keep Sight of What is Important!

*Obviously, positive results are what we're looking for. To
me, the process is what's more important. I think if we
take care of the process then the results will come.*
—Brian Boucher

This chapter is designed to highlight and reinforce key points that could
potentially enhance the results achieved as you perform the sales process.
The following topics are items that I have recently mentioned in the
previous chapter, but I do consider them important enough to review. I
highlight their relevance and value to the process as a reminder that no
matter how simple and obvious they may seem, they do play an important
role, and that they should not be deliberately avoided, or discarded.

SMILE AND KEEP GOOD HUMOR

*A business has to be involving, it has to be fun, and
it has to exercise your creative instincts*
—Richard Branson

Smiling and humor fit in the Creative process. They both work at an emotional level. When combined, these two traits are powerful tools to attract customers. Some clients will be fast to admit that they remain faithful to the same company, or look forward to stopping by the same store time after time, simply because their associates are happy, upbeat, and fun to be around.

If a business owner ever wondered what they could do to exponentially increase sales productivity, the answer would lie in their capacity to provide the employees with an environment in which they are allowed to release stress and develop their creative abilities.

SAS (Tech & Software), Google, and DreamWorks. These companies have something in common. They have been featured as Fortune Magazine's top 10 best companies to work for, mostly because of their creative setting, and because of the many other features, they provide for their employees (http://money.cnn.com/ magazines/fortune/ best companies/2010).

They also have one more thing in common. They all have reached steady and extraordinary success, and are now recognized as some of the most innovative and productive companies in the world. I bring them up to emphasize that the same way the creative standards are a win-win for you and the customer, these companies are proof that the same creative approach is a win-win for the employee and the employer as well. That correlation between happy employees and the remarkable success these companies enjoy is not a product of chance.

The thing about humor is that it can neither be taught, faked nor imitated. Being in an environment that places you in the right frame of mind is the best way to naturally radiate this powerful quality.

Being creative is all about freedom to think and to share ideas, being playful, curious, and spontaneous. Some companies may ask the employee to be creative, productive and to think *outside the box*, but somehow the employee is kept locked inside of it.

It is imperative not to confuse humor with comedy, jokes, or even worse, playing the clown. All of these can be faked, prepared, or flat-out unprofessional. Humor is only relevant when it is sincere, and performed in a relaxed manner that flows with the current conversation or environment. It is impossible to utilize light humor in your favor, if you are uncomfortable, frustrated, stressed, or uninterested.

Regardless of the place of employment, or any other factors, being in a good mood and utilizing light humor in your favor is undoubtedly possible, and a great tool to reaching your personal goals. A few things to remember: Timing is important. Comments have to remain tasteful and professional. Keep loud laughs or extreme mannerism out of the equation. Using your own personal experiences or the customer's previous comments in the conversation is acceptable, if done in a respectful manner… And when in doubt, just smile.

ALWAYS LISTEN

Listening is a magnetic and strange thing, a creative force.
—Karl A. Menninger

Follow-up questions are designed to let the customers express their points of view, while you get the opportunity to gather information necessary to further assist. Their input at any moment in the exchange is very important. However, this dynamic cannot take place, if you do not let them talk!

Based on your own experience, you may be able to recall instances when this has happened. Maybe it was the time you stopped the customer in the middle of a sentence, because you already knew what she was about to ask…or when you asked a question, but kept on talking. Not letting the customer speak and not being able to pause and listen is undoubtedly our most common mistake.

It is true that we think faster than we talk, and many could easily blame this well-known fact, but should that be our excuse? Allow me to answer that for you….No! We shouldn't be making excuses for ourselves when we have the control and knowledge to master such challenges.

Falling into a 'non-listening' pattern may be a combination of lack of awareness and anxiety. If already working under the Creative, this should not be an issue, since under this process you are encouraged to be conscious at all levels. Targeting the negative patterns and focusing your energy on improving them is how awareness plays such an important role.

But whenever you do find yourself in this situation, it is important to remember that some of the strategies found in this book can be of great help. You could for example refer back to the meditation exercise found in Chapter 4. In essence, the inability to pause, either to let the customer answer a question, or just to be still while they take their time to make their point, only happens when you are unable to breathe, remain calm, and be patient. Meditation will help you achieve those goals.

Another tool is the power of affirmations…and why not? They are known to be a great way to change patterns your mind may be working with (Refer to Chapter 5). Believe me, there are no excuses.

POSITIVE WORDS

The power of words is immense. A well-chosen word has often sufficed to stop a flying army, to change defeat into victory, and to save an empire.
—Emile de Girardin

It is simple—You can never go wrong utilizing the right words. You will find a brief list below. Use them to communicate with your clients. They have the positive effect needed to keep them interested. They can highlight the benefits while in your presentation. They can direct attention towards the positive aspects of the product while closing the sale. They can re-establish enough interest for a service or product even after a rejection. They are truly useful at any step of the process...so, use them!

I learned about their importance from one of my favorite co-workers, Max. While on the phone, he would always say things like, "This is a *fabulous* choice." "Wow! It is so *luxurious*!" "You cannot imagine how *awesome* the beach is." I always thought he was so corny—until I saw his paychecks.

AMAZING WONDERFUL BEAUTIFUL LUXURIOUS STUNNING
SPECTACULAR WORTHY REMARKABLE PHENOMENAL
BREATHTAKING UNBELIEVABLE ASTONISHING

ABSOLUTELY SURE NO DOUBT GUARANTEED
REST ASSURED IT IS A FACT BE CERTAIN

TRUSTWORTHY RELIABLE SECURED SAFE TRUSTED
AUTHENTIC DEPENDABLE HONEST RIGHT AWAY IMMEDIATELY
NO WAIT PROMPTLY PRIORITY PUNCTUALLY ON TIME

RISK FREE WORRY FREE WORLD CLASS SERVICE
CONFIDENTIAL PRIVATE EXCLUSIVE

The reality is that words are only words. It is only when infused with emotions that they become relevant. In cases, the very same words you used while you were happy might have had a completely different meaning or interpretation when you were upset. It is by that same application that words take their place in the Creative process.

Under this process, you are aware of their relevance. You know which ones are best to use, and which ones are best to avoid. You are aware enough to know that they must be said with confidence in your product, and with enthusiasm, but most importantly, they must be used only when you believe them to be true and applicable to each particular situation. Using them in any other way will only get you closer to the possibility of breaking that trust.

Unless you have been living under a rock, you have seen an infomercial. It is a $100 billion industry. It generates sales for an infinite variety of products. The success of this industry is based on the combination of positive words, value, and urgency; and while I cannot speak for the veracity or effectiveness of the items or services, I can tell you that this combination works! People are attracted, by the masses, to buying the products offered.

They use expressions such as, *Zero risk guaranteed. Erase all wrinkles and start enjoying beautiful skin. This is a limited offer, only for today, call now! Perfect results every time guaranteed. Do not miss out on this amazing opportunity to get the most effective product on the market.*

It seems as if all they are doing is telling the audience what they want to hear, in a very upbeat way, which is what makes them effective. Our purpose though, is to build a long-term relationship. It is not all about what the customer wants to hear, but how much they can trust what you say.

Always be certain of the veracity of your offer and the quality of your products while presenting them or while making a specific offer. Referrals and repeat customers will bring you a consistent flow of sales and future business…but that could be lost, if they lose confidence in you, or in your products.

WORDS TO AVOID

Handle them carefully, for words have more power than atom bombs.
—Pearl Strachan

I know this to be a fact. You do not want to hear the word *"No"* as a response from your prospect, right? Well, I would recommend you not to use the word *"No"* on the customer either. The same advice applies for the words *cannot, impossible, no way, and forget about it!* There are certain words and expressions that should never be used to respond to the customer's need.

I keep emphasizing the importance of words. In great part, the language you choose will help the customers determine how comfortable or uneasy they feel about you, and about awarding you their business. What you say, and how you say it, will establish the perception of who you are in their minds: rude, nice, sloppy, trustworthy, authoritative, and much more. In other words, what you say could attract them to you, or sadly, the opposite.

The wrong expression could change the flow or outcome of the encounter, even if you didn't intend it. Some conversations can turn confrontational, uncomfortable, and ultimately unprofessional.

No, maybe, and *but*, should not be part of you vocabulary in a business setting. The same way, the following expressions (or those similar) should be avoided while interacting with your customer:

"We can't do that" – "We are busy now" – "It's not my department" – "I don't know" – "I'll let you know later" – "Calm down" – "Like I said…" – "Here's what you are going to do…" – "Call us later" – "You have to…" – "Do you have any problem?" – "I'll try" – "We are not responsible for that"—I'll see what I can do – "Who knows?" "That is against our policy" – "I know I shouldn't be telling you this, but…" – "It's your responsibility" – "It was your fault" – "We don't carry that" – "It's not an option."

Words to avoid include *penalty, impossible, never, problem, difficult, whenever, however, whoever, worthless, uncertain, hopefully,* and as a sign of the times…Never use "LOL" either.

o   "Uh-Huhn" or "Yep" are not a replacement for Yes.

o   "Guys" It's not a formal term to communicate with customers.

o   "What's up!" is not a respectful greeting.

o   "No Problem" is not the reassuring way to solve an issue.

o   "What's wrong?" is not any way to offer your help.

o   "Hold on a sec" is definitely not, what they want to hear.

Use: **Investment** instead of **Budget**

Effort instead of **Struggle**

Value instead of **Price**

Benefits instead of **Features**.

Challenge instead of **Problem**

CHAPTER ELEVEN

Game Changers

Sense of Urgency and Referrals, are two main aspects that could make a great deal of difference in the process. One of them can potentially get you the sale right on the spot, while the other could maintain business flowing back to you in any given moment without much effort. Let's consider them.

CREATE A SENSE OF URGENCY

Procrastination is an issue that can affect even the best of us. At any given moment, it is common to delay doing or getting something, even when we know how important or necessary it is. So I wonder what can lead us to believe that it is any different for our customers. Why should they give out their personal information and credit card numbers to a virtual stranger now, when they can take their sweet time and just wait to do it later? Giving them reasons to close the deal right on the spot, is how you create that sense of urgency. Consider this step...a major game changer.

'I have to think it over' and *'I'll get back to you later,'* are not only some of the most usual excuses, but the hardest to overcome once they have left the customer's mouth. The customer could easily sense your attempt to apply urgency at that point as a gimmick, and in cases, it could just be plain aggravating. When properly applied, however, a sense of urgency can have the opposite effect, increasing your chances of closing the deal faster than you thought.

Creating urgency is not exempt from the use of emotions to trigger a response. People *love* what they cannot have, and *hate* to think they are about to miss out on something—***Love* (Creative) *Hate* (Competitive)**—*keep this in mind.*

Pre-conceived notions would show us the path of the Competitive. Training materials, books and experts alike, agree that the effective emotion is *fear*. They advise us to tap into the fear of loss, calling it *the main motivator in all purchasing decisions*. Some go as far as to say that the most powerful marketing tool is *scarcity*, and *limited supply*; and don't forget about well-known techniques that threaten with fees and penalties. (…And I wondered why I was never inspired).

The world is changing. September 11 got us to unite and get closer to our families-—The economic downturn came later, and got us closer to our wallets. People are learning to get priorities straight. Consumer's purchasing impulses are not at the level they used to be. The pressure from the sales person is bound to be rather annoying, and it does not change the new realities.

Consumers are making greater strides to become more educated. No doubt, technology and mass media makes it even easier. Don't forget, *"There's an app for that!"* All it takes is just one click and a few minutes to research any product or service, and compare prices and availability. In other words, that customer standing in front of you may be the savvy kind. The type that is aware of the traditional selling techniques and ready to be assertive…and with good reason.

The negative effects of working under the Competitive tend to snowball. It is common to rush, warn, and push, just to have customers come back with complaints, rather than new business. Some customers trusted when told it was a *"limited offer"* or *"For today only,"* just to find out a month later, that it was still available. Others were told, *"Price will increase very soon"* or, *"Buy now, this is the last one at this low price"* to find out a few days later that the price had actually gone down.

I remind you of my early emphasis—Whether you stand on the Creative or Competitive, there is no doubt that achieving success is possible. The question is how hard or easy you want it to be. I assure you I understand that some of the best sales professionals and companies in the world use the tactics outlined above with great success. However, while it is completely true that people hate to miss out on opportunities, and that they are fearful of limited supply, I remind you that fear, scarcity, limitation and even threats have no place in the Creative.

***Love* (Creative) *Hate* (Competitive)**—So, how do we proceed without dwelling on the Competitive? How can we effectively create urgency and apply those well-known techniques recently mentioned, without breaking the customer's trust? After all, based on my previous point, *love* and *hate* do seem to go hand in hand in this topic.

The key lies in *desire*. It is strategic to keep in mind that desire grows stronger when we fear we cannot have something; however, instead of highlighting the *fear*, under the Creative process I encourage you to highlight the *desire*.

People often respond more favorably to feelings of desire, rather than need. How many times have you been to The Home Depot in search of something you desperately need: light bulbs, a new doorknob, mop, and bucket? Instead, you came out with new lamps, vases, area rugs, and ten square feet of that fantastic tile, that would look great as a backdrop in your kitchen. A week later, you still cannot get into that closet at night because it is still too dark; you are worried that your back door is unsafe, and let's not talk about those floors. There was no fun buying mop and bucket, but the thought of refreshing the kitchen and having the compliments of the friends visiting next month, sounded great.

I remember how a few years ago, some of my acquaintances looked as if they had just come out of an episode of *Miami Vice*. They were walking around with cell phones that were, for lack of a better word... pretty basic. If you ever dared to ask why they would still carry such outdated devices, they would look at you as if you were the one with the issues. They would reply something like, *"What else do you need a telephone for, if it is not to make a call? This one serves its purpose, thank you very much!"*

They were certainly in need of new cell phones. They had 21st Century professions; they needed devices that matched the era. However, all efforts were futile; even the ones that instilled fear of missing business due to the inability to check e-mails right on the spot, or the urgency to buy them soon, not to miss out on some of the unbelievable promotions all major cell phone companies were advertising at that particular time.

Well, at least I was able to see firsthand the case of one of them who changed his mind after his wife got the iPhone in the early stages of its release. His wife, also concerned with his lack of interest, allowed him to borrow it for a few days on purpose.

After only three days, he wondered how he could ever have lived without some of the features; but he explained that what really made him change his mind, were all the compliments he got at work. He explained that some of his coworkers were somewhat jealous that he was able to get his hands on one before they did.

It is obvious that envy and admiration from his coworkers created enough desire for him to completely change his mind and invest in something that he now calls "a necessity"… Wasn't that the same thing we were trying to tell him from the beginning?!

Customers step into our places of business with a 'want' and/or a 'need.' Our task is to keep the momentum going to the point that there is no other alternative for the customer than leaving the store with that they came looking for…or something comparable. This can be accomplished by giving them the many reason why that item or service is what they want, need, or what they are simply looking for. Incorporate along with those facts, the reasons why they will not regret that purchase.

Consider those kinds of comments and explanations a reinforcement that can be implemented at any moment of the process. You are undoubtedly giving your clients the reassurance that it is okay to make a purchasing decision right on the spot. On the other hand, your customer could sense information about limited supply, limited-time offers, and special pricing, as a gimmick. Regrettably, this type of information is easily misused, and when that happens, the best you could get out of them is a fast deal. So, to avoid that…below are some examples of the proper ways to highlight the *desire*.

o   Emphasize the exclusivity of the item. If applicable, inform how the customer is among the first wave of people buying it.

o   Compliment them on their choice and go as far as explaining why it is such a good decision to buy now. This may automatically put down major doubts they had about making the purchase. (*"This is a very smart decision…."*)

o Talk about the great experience others have had with the product, and comment on all the positive feedback you have received. That would not only lower the likelihood that they have to hold off while they check reviews, but it would also have them wondering, *why wait!*"

o Point out all the reasons why they need to have that item *now*, such as popularity, quality, promotions, and special offers available at that time.

o Remind them of all the great benefits they can start enjoying right away, such as ownership, envy, comfort, luxury, and more (*"You can leave the parking lot driving your own brand new car right now!"*).

o Mention the fact that a great number of clients are calling or stopping by to buy the product. (*"Flying off the shelves."*)

o Provide factual information on why buying now is the right thing to do. (*"It is very smart to make the reservation this early. July is peak-season. Prices are bound to increase soon)*

o Highlight the assumption of the status the purchase brings, like the fact that only a certain group of people can get it, due to special memberships, rank, seniority, or location.

o If applicable, represent the product as the 'must have' item of the season. Use this one especially if at any moment of the discovery step you sensed the client to be the trendy type.

ASKING FOR REFERRALS

Among sales professionals, there is no better feeling than the one we get when closing a deal we didn't have to work for, right? Well, technically, we did work for it, and probably hard; however, there is no doubt that there is a certain satisfaction to being on the receiving end of positive sales experiences. It feels like being in cruise control. That is undoubtedly one of the benefits of referrals. They give you the great advantage of increasing both, revenue and closing ratio, without much extra effort.

Referrals however, will not take place until a certain level of trust is established. And that brings the emphasis back to one of the themes in this book—the importance of following a specific pattern to build not only valuable trust between you and your customer, but also the higher value found in not breaking that trust at any point in the process.

Have you ever heard anybody say, *"I'll send you to my guy?"* They are talking about their favorite sales person. They know that person will make them look good, and there is a sense of pride in that. Referrals are produced by word of mouth. Capitalized upon by some of the most successful companies and sales people, word of mouth is considered one of the best marketing techniques. And why not! It is effective. It is easy…and it is free.

The step-by-step process outlined on Chapter 9 is designed with referrals in mind. Properly followed, it will give you the advantage needed to increase not only your chances of closing the sale, but the chances to close future transactions as well. Remember how I mentioned the importance of providing the customer with your business card, and how I advised you to create the connection right from the greeting where you can easily add, *"I will be your personal consultant, and from now on, I'm the person to contact for all your future needs. You can reach me at…"*

…But while the right strategies and an overall good experience will always leave the door open for future referrals, it is also very appropriate to actively ask for them.

Timing is important. It is precisely at the end of the process, while you are facing a satisfied customer, that asking for referrals makes sense, and it is highly recommended. At that moment, you can re-assure your customers that it will be your pleasure to take care of their friends and family, the same way you just took care of them.

On occasions, I have even asked my clients to post my card on their refrigerator door. They always laugh; but I wasn't kidding. I really meant for them to post my card on their refrigerator.

Not being able to consciously ask for referrals raises a red flag; it should be one of the greatest signals that you are still working under the wrong process. There are many reasons why a number of sales professionals do not seem to take advantage of this helpful feature:

o They are *afraid* to ask (Fear)

o They *feel uncomfortable* (Uncertainty)

o They *forget* to do it (Dismissal)

o They *feel* they are *begging* for business (Ego)

o They *do not believe* it is effective or even necessary (Lack of confidence).

Look at the keywords that identify each one of the reasons why the sales person fails to ask for referrals. By now, you know that those values belong with the Competitive process. It is not a matter of being robotic or 'pushing' yourself to do it; it is a matter of placing yourself within the right process. One in which you are able to reach the opposite mindset that makes you aware of the relevance of every single one of the elements found in sales. One in which you get enough confidence to naturally perform and excel.

In the end, the equation is simple:

$$BS+BE=H2R$$

(Bad Service + Bad Experience = Hard to Return)

$$GS+GE=S2R$$

(Good Service + Good Experience = Sure to Return)

CHAPTER TWELVE

Knowledge

Our ability to achieve depends on the strength of our wings gained through knowledge and experience. The greater our knowledge and experience, the higher we can fly.

—Catherine Pulsifer

Your experience, skills, education, and practical understanding of the information related to your product and your field will not only set you apart, but it will also give you greater advantage over others. It is, however, not only what you know, but also how you use it to your advantage that truly makes the difference, and that has the potential to place you in creative mode.

Whoever said *knowledge is power* was onto something. The statement has great meaning in the business world, where we can clearly see that the most successful individuals are those who improved their skills and are now able to master their craft—becoming innovators and leaders of the pack.

There should be no doubt that the benefits of *knowledge* are of vital importance in the sales field, as well. Information and leadership skills are bound to be assets for any of us on any given day. Nonetheless, the most important benefit to us as individuals in the Creative Process should always be *confidence*.

Synonyms of the word confidence include self-assurance, self-belief, and self-reliance. The meaning of the word *confidence* is closely related to the meaning of the word knowledge; after all, it was Plato's description of the word knowledge, *"justified true belief"*. Confidence is belief and trust… the kind that you apply within yourself and in your abilities.

Customers can easily sense the confidence within you because of the way you present your ideas and products, but mostly, in the authority you exude when you address and solve their specific needs.

Everybody gravitates toward the person with the most authority or knowledge in the field. When vacationing on a cruise ship, the person passengers most want to meet is the captain; when reading that book you love, no doubt there is always a desire to meet the author; when buying a painting, who is best to explain its real meaning or significance than the artist himself?

Knowledge gives you the authority and edge that everybody values and respects. Confidence, however, gives you the power to demonstrate that knowledge…and achieving it will only be possible with awareness.

There are countless cases of people knowledgeable enough to write a book or two, but still not able to accomplish much in their respective fields. This is due to lack of consciousness and purpose. We must be willing to leave our comfort zone and become aware of our assets. Only then, will we be capable of directing them.

Aspiring job candidates are shocked to learn that after much preparation and time spent in learning technical information related to the industry and/or company they are applying to, they did not pass the test. After so much preparation, they were rejected and another applicant with more aptitude was chosen…but was it really aptitude or having more knowledge that got that other person the job? What could have really set them apart?

The answer is that without exuding confidence you won't be able to give others any reasons to put trust in your own capabilities, since you yourself don't seem able to do that. Lack of confidence does not shadow your knowledge or similar other qualities, but it does tell others that you may not be ready to put them to use in a way that could maximize results.

Whoever said, knowledge *IS* power, was really onto something. He or she very accurately used the verb *to be*, but without the capacity to bring forth meaningful abilities from within our **be**ing, we come to realize that even power can be useless when not properly applied, and knowledge stripped away from those vital abilities will no longer be power, it would just be…well, knowledge.

CHAPTER THIRTEEN

Believe

*Keep your dreams alive. Understand to achieve anything requires
faith and belief in yourself, vision, hard work, determination, and
dedication. Remember all things are possible for those who believe.*
—Gail Devers

FAITH (n.) – At the core of the Creative process, is faith. It would be
safe to describe it as the power that allows for expansion and fulfillment.
Without it, our efforts are in vain. What is a car with no engine or a tree
without roots? If you can answer that, you will be able to find answers
regarding what the Creative process is without faith.

There is no purpose in visualizing, if you do not believe in your
dreams, or setting goals without the confidence that they can be reached.
What is the purpose of repeating affirmations with no expectation of
change or improvement? And what can I tell you about prayer? Faith is
the substance that moves it all and makes it all work, just like the engine
beneath the hood of your car—-you don't doubt the car will propel you

forward once you push the pedal, because, even though you cannot see it, you know it is there.

The definition of the word *polarity* (http://dictionary.reference.com/browse/polarity) indicates the presence or manifestation of two opposite or contrasting principles or tendencies. Two poles standing, one in front of each other. They do not touch. You are on either one side or the other. You are not on both at the same time. The point is that it is not possible to be in the Creative and in the Competitive at the same time. Once you waiver or doubt one process, you have entered into its opposite.

Faith is the conviction that something is possible even with no proof of existence. Creation is the act of bringing forth what is not yet in existence. They both go hand in hand.

It is here that I warn you, though, that the qualities that stem from faith are invaluable; therefore, they have great potential to *propel* you further than your desk or office. Side effects include, but are not limited to enhanced self-esteem, confidence, loyalty, commitment, dedication, conviction, vision, and sense of purpose—all words associated with the term.

BELIEVE (v.) – It is time to put your faith into action, and believe. Believing is an act that stems from your heart and from your mind… an action that nobody else can perform for you. If you don't believe in yourself, who else would? If you can't believe in your dreams, who else can? Believe in the possibilities as you visualize them. Believe in your abilities as you get the knowledge. Believe in The Higher Source as you pray. And always, believe in yourself.

I would like to share with you the eight simple words of my favorite scripture in the Bible:

Be still and know that I am God.
Psalm 46:10 (KJV)

It is amazing how so few words can say so much. The Creator, Himself, is asking us *not* to be anxious, and to put *faith* in Him. We are being asked to *be still*, which in a few words describes the main purpose of *meditation*. The act of *prayer* is involved as the ultimate way to connect, while other abilities like *knowledge* and *confidence* are very much implied. It seems as if all the major qualities leading to the Creative are 'bundled up into one all-inclusive package' (no pun intended).

In an effort to present one of the most fitting examples of our time, I will now turn the focus to Dr. Martin Luther King. His legacy is a reminder that true creative people are always relevant… even in the darkest hour. In fact, it is at the lowest moment when they raise, act, and make a real difference in the world. We can easily identify them because of their vision, their *dreams*, their passion, and their *faith*.

"Almost always, the creative dedicated minority
has made the world better."
—Martin Luther King, Jr.

We know that faith is their primary value simply because they can very accurately give us a description of what faith, or being creative means in just a few words. Dr. King was a leader, an activist, a man of action and change, yet his legacy is one of hope and inspiration, and the perfect example of why faith is in fact the substance that could drive us all to keep moving forward…even if it is just one-step at the time.

"Faith is taking the first step, even when you don't see the whole staircase."
—Martin Luther King, Jr.

Based on my early "theories," opposites will always be present. I previously mentioned how you cannot be in one pole and expect to experience the results belonging to its opposite. It is imperative to function within the one process that is *positive* 'by nature.' Well, it is through Martin Luther King's own words and by the words of the few just like him that we get a window into their minds, and into what is truly possible. His, however, was not a theory. His course of action was rather based on *justified true belief.* With a specific cause in mind, one that he truly believed in; and with the right set of values, he was empowered to change the course of an entire nation.

*"**Darkness** cannot drive out darkness; only **light** can do that.*
***Hate** cannot drive out hate; only **love** can do that."*
—Martin Luther King, Jr.

Whether it is a social cause or just a specific set of daily targets and goals, consider faith one of your greatest assets to achieve each one of them. Make faith your primary value, and find out how far you can go. The results may surprise you. After all, the car cannot function without the engine. The tree cannot grow without roots. We cannot perform in the Creative without faith. So go ahead, and believe!

MY BREAKOUT

My all-time favorite pastime was with the weekend newspaper. I used to get up in the morning to get a hold of it before anybody else, just to make a whole lot of mess taking it apart to find my favorite section. I was ten. My parents soon decided to outsmart me by getting up even earlier and hiding it from me. I started finding the section I wanted below my cereal bowl every Saturday; I knew then, the weekend had arrived.

Back then, I had no interest in world news or politics. All I wanted was the Comics section. The cartoons were fun, but what I really enjoyed the most was a black and white drawing that took almost a quarter of the page under the title, *What's Wrong With This Picture?* It showed a seemingly normal scenario, but warned that it was not what it appeared to be. The task was to find ten things that were wrong in the drawing. Over time, I got good at it, and it was getting easier to complete each time.

So, why, if I was so good at finding the *wrongs* in a cartoon drawing, wasn't I fast enough to realize what was wrong in my own real-life approach? Many years later, I was given another chance to play the game; the major difference was that this time around, I wasn't having as much fun with it. I have taken a genuine look back to that day in June, and realized that what seemed normal on the surface actually had many wrongs.

'The picture' is described in the introduction of this book where I recounted that eventful day in June. I started by saying, I had no plans or expectations, which translates into no goals and into no major objectives to meet. I described how I rushed out the door, which automatically places me on the wrong side of the spectrum; and to top it all, my focus was mostly placed on the barrage of negative news I had heard on the radio that morning, in an effort to keep up with a declining economy. We now know that placing focus on externals will in-turn generate a reaction (worry, stress, limitation…). I guess I should get points for getting up on the right side of the bed; at least, that showed some type of effort to ensure a good day.

In the next paragraphs, I explained how the atmosphere at work was fun, and how I handled all competition and challenges thrown my way to the best of my abilities. What was wrong with that? I was working hard, and facing the environment head-on, as I should…right? What do awareness and consciousness have to do with it anyway?

Well, let me ask you, have you ever seen a lemming? In case you wonder what they look like, at only 5 inches long, it is a real-life size Zhu-Zhu Pet™ (In stores everywhere).

These tiny creatures reproduce very quickly. They breed from spring to fall, and in favorable years, even in winter. In response to the overcrowding, they begin to migrate from the center of the dense population grouped together, following each other. Whatever barriers block their passage they tend to crowd in increasing numbers until a sort of panic reaction pushes them over the obstacles.

Once watching an animal kingdom channel, I came across a documentary about this little animal. I learned that the migration impulse affects each individual, driving them to keep moving. If a stream or river interrupts their path, they swim across. Many die during migration, perishing by predation, starvation, or accident. Occasionally, some reach the ocean and plunge in. Once in the ocean they keep-on swimming, driven by the same impulse that drove them to cross the smaller bodies of water. Swimming until exhausted, all of them drown.

I love animal shows; but this is truly a sad tale. Scientists have not yet been able to discover why these migrations have taken place for centuries, with the same end result. The theory is that there is a moment when the lemming forgets about the original idea of food, and becomes the victim of a one-track thought; and with no other specific goal in mind, it just keeps moving, mindlessly following the crowd, even when it means jumping off a cliff.

Other theories implying that the lemming becomes suicidal have been discarded over the years since specialists have concluded that the original thought that drove them to migrate was *limited* supply, and nothing else. Bottom line, this little rodent may not be aware that anything is wrong, until is too late.

What was truly interesting is that the same documentary showed what seemed to be endless images of the vast Tundra of Alaska—which is where this little rodent is found. At no time did their habitat show any signs of lack of roots, moss, or grass, which are their main source of food. I personally wondered what if they were to stop for a moment to become aware of their surroundings. Those able to do that could lead the rest in breaking out of the pack, and heading in the opposite direction with more intention. Maybe then, they could find food beyond their wildest dreams; but maybe, I thought, they just don't know any better.

Lemmings might seem to be mere creatures that do not have much purpose and cannot possibly teach us anything, but nature is a magnificent teacher. Nature is always talking to us through the smallest and seemingly insignificant things; and there is no doubt that those who listen are bound to benefit abundantly.

I know now that instead of applying thought and awareness, I was following the crowd and all pre-conceived notions; and as a result, I found myself drowning in exhaustion and stress. It wasn't until I stopped for a moment and took some time to think and breathe that I was able to break out and find a place in which I am now comfortable enough to smile and succeed in a greater way.

Will this be your break out year? Only you can answer that. I remind you however, that there are always possibilities for both, limitation and abundance. There is an option that will lead to the positive and one leading toward the negative. There is a way to make it flow and another one sure to involve struggle. Each option is at your fingertips—it is your choice.

It took long enough, but that is precisely the one factor that has put all my theories together—*Freedom of will*. As previously stated, both approaches might be innate elements of our being; therefore, positive and negative will always be there, just like in any common battery, or any other artificial energy source. Do we naturally lean toward the positive pole, or is it the tendency to gravitate automatically toward the negative? Whichever process or course of action you choose to follow is how you measure that tendency.

Sometimes we make decisions unaware of how one seemingly simple act can affect many areas of our lives. What is truly interesting is that life is full of those choices. Therefore, the way we face everyday decisions…whether we choose to act or react, and the choices we make in a day-to-day basis, will become the defining elements of our true direction in life.…regardless of the profession.

Take for example the one occupation that could take you the farthest away from the dreaded sales cubicle…thousands of miles away…up in *the sky*, attending to passengers. In the face of a situation considered by any standards a major anxiety trigger… would you be the kind of person who could breathe, focus within, and push forward with a good attitude? Or would you be the one who kicks open the emergency door and jumps off the plane at the first chance you have while sounding off a loud…*"I quit"*?

I did the latter…and many people in this country fall victim to the same split-second insanity (Just log on to YouTube. You may encounter the case of Steven Slater, the infamous ex-JetBlue employee). If the stressful environment were truly here to stay, the lemming-like behavior could become something more common to read about in the daily news, or to see in our own workplaces…not just in the animal kingdom shows. Times are changing. It only makes sense to change with the times.

Once a rocket is launched from NASA's Cape Kennedy, bound for space beyond our sky, there is no limit to where it can go. The target may be the moon, or depending on technology and purpose, even farther away. The same happens in your mind. Once you have made a decision, you can shoot for the moon, and as the popular saying goes, *"even if you miss, you will be among the stars,"* in any case, you would have reached stunning heights not possible in any other way. I once heard someone say, *the only real limitations are the ones you set upon yourself,* and with that in mind, you could soon also realize that just as the sky has no limits, neither do you.

….And that is my case.

I now have to go and tell my husband I wrote half of a book based on him. In the meantime, I hope that this book can be of assistance to you and to those with whom you decide to share it.

APPENDIX A

The Basis for the Two Processes and the Bible Principles that Support the Theory [The Case]

I know this world is ruled by infinite intelligence. Everything that surrounds us- everything that exists - proves that there are infinite laws behind it. There can be no denying this fact. It is mathematical in its precision.
—Thomas A. Edison

When you hear about Quantum Law or the Law of Gravity, do you have any doubts that they exist? Most likely, the answer is, *no*. The two terms have something in common. They are both fundamental laws of nature. The concepts of infinite intelligence and the Laws of the Universe however, do constantly meet a challenge. They are accepted [believed] by some, and disregarded [denied] by others. But if the statement, *there are laws of the universe*, were true, one might ask, *Who created them?*

Based on practicality, it is safe to say that explosions or some big bang, in general do not set laws; and the evolutionary process of apes can certainly not establish them either. Laws are set by a Master—one with enough authority and power to institute them with the purposes of organization and order. If the so-called laws of the universe do in fact exist, then it makes sense that there should be a process, set to follow the guidelines of those laws.

So based on that, those who make the conscious decision to ignore the Creator [of those laws] may achieve the success they sought, and at times, the kind that is beyond their wildest dreams. However, ignoring the path [process] that acknowledges that Creator [Creative] means that the *opposite route [Competitive]* was taken, and it is one of the purposes of this book to highlight the benefits and disadvantages found in following each process, as well as the *results* and consequences that could eventually leave us asking…'*Was it worth it?*'

From the early sections of this book, I mentioned that the 'law' and concepts of the *case at hand* are laid in the Bible. This appendix is designed with the purpose to support that statement. The Bible principles substantiate the information found within the pages of this book. Consider this your bird's eye view of how it all connects.

So place your focus, for a moment, on how all things with no exemption follow a set pattern, and nothing escapes it. Our experiences and possibilities are no doubt finite; we can accomplish and create abundantly; however, everything accomplished is unquestionably within a realm, and nobody seems to be immune to it.

> "*For He will not lay upon man more than right; that*
> *he should enter into judgment with God*"
> –Job 34:23

"Do you know the laws of the universe? Can
you use them to regulate the earth?"
Job 38:33 NLT

Look at the news. Look at the world. Look around you. Notice how
a behavior always has an effect. A situation generates an experience.
Thoughts bring forth ideas, words, and actions; and no matter how
small and insignificant it may seem, notice how those actions have
repercussions (results). What you say matters; how you act affects yourself
and others. In other words, your choices influence the outcome. This
affects each human being on the planet no matter how far or close, or
how high or low we come from. It sounds like a system put in place.

What you say matters—*"Death and life are in the power of the tongue."*
—Proverbs 18:21 NAS
What you do matters/ Results (fruits): *"Say you to the righteous, that it*
shall be well with him, for they shall eat the fruit of their doings."
—Isaiah 3:10 AKJV
When doing right, good happens—*"Do good, O LORD, unto those*
that be good, and to them that are upright in their hearts."
—Psalms 125:4 WEB
When doing wrong, we get wrong—*"Certainly the one that is doing*
wrong will receive back what he wrongly did, and there is no partiality."
—Colossians 3:25 NWT
Thoughts produce actions—*"For from within, out of the heart of men,*
proceed evil thoughts, sexual immorality, theft, murders..."
—Mark 7:21 NIV

Look at your body. Averaging only 5 to 6 feet tall, the human body is
so intricate and complex, that one could go to school for three to four
years straight and we would still not be able to learn the half of it. Proof
is that doctors, spend more than that only to specialize in one area. Yet,
how is it possible that the billions of us on the face of this planet are all

built the same identical way? Our physical traits are different. Skin color, height, width, and appearance will distinguish us from one another, but the blueprint is identical. A Bang or an explosion implies a whole lot of mess, but the way we are all *built*... sure looks more like a design.

"I will praise thee; for I am fearfully and wonderfully made..."
Psalms 139:14 KJV

The same model of how we are all similarly built externally, applies internally as well. I am referring now to the very essence of our being. After all, we obviously never hear on the news that somebody grew, or bought a new set of feelings that any of us doesn't already possess. That is because we have all been equally endowed with a full array of them, deeply ingrained within us. When something is right, you know it is right because you can sense the appropriate emotions arising from within as spontaneously as the sunrise. On the other hand, when a situation is negative, uncomfortable, or just plain wrong, the perception is opposite. (Even when we don't know what to think, we may sense what Oprah calls the *"Aha! moment"*). Our feelings are there all the time; they never leave us. We are the ones who make the decision to abandon what they are trying to tell us, in an effort to react to the situation, as fast as it happens, without much thought.

".... What helpful insight you have abundantly provided!"
Job 26:3 NAS

It does not stop there. According to the Bible, the Creator also provides talents. If you are thinking of Lady Gaga, you may not be far from the truth. The Bible knew far ahead that those gifts would make room for them in the world to become important people, and to meet even greater ones; like the Queen of England, for example. Who could forget that red dress Ms. Gaga wore to meet the queen? It was fierce!

"Every good and perfect gift is from above, coming down from the Father of the heavenly lights, who does not change like shifting shadows."
James 1:17 NIV

"A man's gift makes room for him, and brings him before great men."
Proverbs18:16 AKJV

Everything comes with a purpose. Every part of our body has a function, every situation we go through has a rationale; every talent or gift has an intention. Even all the built-in features of our planet seemed to have been conveniently positioned for our enjoyment and satisfaction. To try to rationalize all the beauty, wonder, glory, magnificence, splendor, and intricate design of everything that we enjoy, and replace them with apes and Bangs, in order to provide explanation, fact, or science, could show our own resistance to change...or to simply believe.

"For the invisible things of him from the creation of the world are clearly seen, being understood by the things that are made, even his eternal power and Godhead; so that they are without excuse: Because that, when they knew God, they glorified him not as God, neither were thankful; but became vain in their imaginations and their foolish heart was darkened. Professing themselves to be wise, they became fools, and changed the glory of the incorruptible God into an image made like to corruptible man, and to birds, and four-footed beasts, and creeping things."
Romans 1:20-23 KJV

...But that is the exact same principle that applies to the Creative and the Competitve. You see, one of the concepts is based on provision, faith, abundance, and a design that goes further than our sight and power; while the opposite concept is based on the externals, and in the constant need to label, control, and provide explanation for our experiences. Using its own proper terminology, these two *opposite* processes are evidently found in the Bible, and they are illustrated as *Spiritual* (inner) and *Flesh* (external).

> *"For the flesh sets its desire against the Spirit, and the Spirit against the flesh; for these are in opposition to one another..."*
> Galatians 5:17 NAS

Sky is the Limit highlights the influence of both processes from an emotional level. In review, while The Creative involves qualities that include, passion, faith, peace, kindness and self-awareness, the opposite process, the Competitive, involves strife, envy, jealousy, comparison, and on occasions, even outbursts of anger or plain frustration.

> *"Now the deeds of the **flesh** are evident, which are: immorality, impurity, sensuality, idolatry, sorcery, enmities, **strife**, **jealousy**, **outbursts of anger**, **disputes**, **dissensions**, factions, **envying**, drunkenness, carousing, and things like these, of which I forewarn you, just as I have forewarned you, that those who practice such things will not inherit the kingdom of God. But the fruit of the **Spirit** is **love**, **joy**, **peace**, **patience**, **kindness**, goodness, **faithfulness**, gentleness, **self-control**..."*
> Galatians 5:19-23 NAS

Sky is the Limit also highlights the main actions that fall within each process. It is clear now that working within competitive standards, does not leave much room for cooperation and teamwork. It becomes second nature to judge and compare...and challenging one another for bragging rights is just part of the 'game.' Against all this, the Bible also counsels.

> *"Let us not become boastful, challenging one another, envying one another."*
> Galatians 5:26 NAS

On the other hand, the Creative is driven by a completely different set of standards. Going back to the times of creation, in the book of Genesis, we notice how at the beginning there was direct communication between God and man. The fact that God does not physically talk to us now may not mean that He lost power; it may rather mean He wants to test ours. *Faith, resistance, knowledge* are just some of the few ones we find referenced in the Bible. Some dictionaries describe faith as the **power** to believe, and resistance as the **power** to oppose or withstand. Don't forget the expression, knowledge is **power** …and even Celine sings to the **power** of love.

> *"Blessed is the man who perseveres under trial, because*
> *when he has stood the test, he will receive the crown of*
> *life that God has promised to those who love him."*
> James1:12 NIV

…And that is precisely what makes the Creative possible—Power! Not only the kind that we exude, utilize, and is sensed by others by the way we perform, but the kind of power that we keep within us that can help us deal with situations and make us stronger. As previously stated in this book, *if you don't keep your power within, you will be more susceptible to setbacks and breakdowns.*

> *"If thou lose hope being weary in the day of distress,*
> *thy strength shall be diminished."*
> Proverbs 24:10 DRA

Using the power of the Creative is right. Especially because, when properly performed, the opposite process is not part of it. In other words, while working under the Creative influence, the results are commonly positive. Even when at times we didn't reach a particular goal, under this process that would not be considered a failure; it would only be considered another *stepping-stone* for what is ahead. Remember, the Creative is marked by *faith*; and the Competitive by *fear*. You cannot have faith and fear at the same time. If you did, it would only mean that you never loved (passion), believed, hoped, envisioned, or any of the qualities that belong to the process.

"There is no fear in love. But perfect love drives out fear, because fear has to do with punishment. The one who fears is not made perfect in love."
1 John 4:18 NIV

The concept of the Creative being involved in our professional lives and financial matters may not be the most common route. Many tend to think that those are matters left alone for church and Sundays. It may be time to recognize that the Creative welcomes us every day, and encourages us to excel; but what makes the process even more effective is that with simple changes you can automatically experience its positive effects. In sales, this process will in part encourage us to be in harmony with the needs of others, compelling us to improve even for a moment, the lives of those around us. You will realize that the more people you serve, the higher your earning potential. Millionaires and successful business people did not attain wealth by buying their own products… they had to serve others first. Or like Zig Ziglar would say, *"You can have everything in life you want, if you will just help other people get what they want."*

"Do not merely look out for your own personal interests, but also for the interests of others."
Philippians 2:4 NAS

"…If anyone would be first, he must be last of all and servant of all."
Mark 9:35 ESV

The opposite process, the Competitive, focuses on 'materials' instead. The spotlight is placed on [external] desires and targets—including profits, position, status, and even the instant gratification of a sales transaction. (As stated in this book, those who are truly successful credit the love for what they do *first!* Fame and fortune just seem to follow). It is the objective of those under the influence of the Competitive, to *do what it takes* to reach a certain purpose, even if it means working tirelessly. And with goal(s) in mind, rivalry, envy, comparison, and a desire to make-it faster, higher and better are all placed in motion. As a result, stress, worry and fear, become natural aspects of that process.

"Then I saw that all hard work and skillful effort come from rivalry. Even this is pointless. It's like trying to catch the wind."
Ecclesiastes 4:4 GW

Was it all worth it? That is the question! Could the Bible be right when it implies the results obtained at the end of this process would make it all…*pointless?* Well, let us look at the big picture. If you want to see the effects, and results of working within the Competitive on a grander scale, all you have to do is turn to the media. It is filled with news of people who in their race to gain riches first, displayed greed, deception, and complete disregard for others; leaving behind a trail of damage. Enron and Maddoff, are words that could put a face to it all, however, the list of people caught committing fraud, and others on the receiving end of it, is virtually endless. Suicide and life in prison are some of the most common results or consequences for those facing ruin and bankruptcy, due to the pursuit of their own desires, and the quality of their very own decisions; while the hurt and pain of others on the receiving end, affected by these individuals and organizations, is undoubtedly immeasurable.

"Those who desire to be rich fall into temptation, into a snare, into many senseless and harmful desires that plunge people into ruin and destruction. For the love of money is a root to all kinds of evil. It is through this craving that some have wandered away from the faith and pierced themselves with many pangs."
1 Timothy 6: 9-10 ESV

I will close with one last thought....the message I found in the Bible is that the Creator wants us to be triumphant, victorious... or better yet, in sales jargon, He literally wants us to be *"the top dog."* Truth be told, His Holy Word is directed toward higher goals and purposes, such as the Kingdom and eternal life, but the information is practical and relevant to our modern-day lives, and it could only be considered wise to at least try to reflect on it, or to be open to it.

"God will make you the head, not the tail; you will always be the top dog, never the bottom dog."
Deuteronomy 28:13 MES

APPENDIX B

Bible Version Abbreviations

ASV—American Standard Version

AKJV – American King James Version

DRA – Douay-Rheims American Edition

ESV – English Standard Version

GW –God's Word

KJV – King James Version

MES – The Message

NAB – New American Bible

NAS – New American Standard Bible

NEB – New English Bible

NIV –New International version

NKJV—New King James Version

NWT – New World Translation

WEB—Webster Bible